C000253770

ALPHA MALE
STRATEGIES
ADVANCED GAME

ALPHA MALE STRATEGIES
ADVANCED GAME

How to Maintain the Attachment in the Social Media Age

BY

ALPHA MALE STRATEGIES

© 2019 by Alpha Male Strategies

All rights reserved. This book or any portion thereof may not be reproduced or used in any manner whatsoever without the express written permission of the publisher except for the use of brief quotations in a book review.

Introduction

Welcome to my second installment about obtaining the woman and lifestyle you want to obtain and my third book overall. This book picks up where my first book, the best-selling *Alpha Male Strategies: Dating in the Social Media Age*, left off. We all know how hard it is to get a woman's attention in the social media age thanks to social media, but once you've gotten her attention and built an attachment, it takes just as much skill to maintain that attachment. This is why I'm writing this book. Before I go any further in this book, I want to warn you: I will not be going over the basics of game in this book. The basics, as I like to call them, are how to become a high-value male, to develop an abundance mind-set, and to develop and maintain a masculine frame. I go into detail on these three things in my first book, *Alpha Male Strategies: Dating in the Social Media Age*. If you haven't developed those three basic skills I teach, then this book won't work for you because it's written with the understanding that you have fully grasped those areas of your life. Without those three things being in place, you won't maintain any woman's interest very long. If you haven't read *Alpha Male Strategies: Dating in the Social Media Age*, then I suggest you read it first before going any further. This book will be more geared toward developing and maintaining an attachment, whereas my first book was more geared toward developing yourself and the right mind-set to lose your weakness for women.

Women Control the Pace Initially

A lot of men get frustrated with the way dating dynamics are set up in the beginning. A man has to make the approach, the man has to ask the woman out, and the man has to hope that the woman will give him a second date—all while the woman sits back and decides if she wants to give you her number, if she wants to go on a date with you, if she wants to go on a second date with you, and whether sex takes place. It's safe to say women do the choosing, but why is it that way? Women do the choosing because men are usually sold on a woman's beauty, while women are sold on a man's personality, confidence, and strength. You can say confidence and strength are in the same boat because a man doesn't have strength without confidence. If a man doesn't believe 100 percent in his abilities to replace a woman, he won't be able to show strength. Even if you wait for choosing signals, it's highly unlikely the woman pursues you, because feminine energy is not aggressive energy. Men have to pursue in the beginning because aggressiveness is a sign of masculine energy, which is attractive. Have you ever wondered why a woman who is overpursuing you from the start usually turns you off despite you having a high physical attraction? It's because if you're a masculine man, a woman displaying that same energy is a turnoff. It's OK for a woman to pursue you, which could be her initiating a text once a week to tell you good morning, but a woman texting you every morning to tell you good morning the first week you met her is always a turnoff. Unlike why this behavior turns a woman off, which is because it shows low sexual market value, masculine energy just isn't attracted to more masculine energy. Be that as it may, as with pretty much anything dealing with the mating dynamics between a man and a woman, eventually the men have the last laugh. While women may control the pace initially, men eventually control the pace. A man controls the pace at which he and the woman get into a relationship or marriage if you're the marriage type. This only applies to high-value men, however. Low-value men propose to women in the hope of making a woman love them forever. Low-value men propose to women, even though the woman has even sent passive-aggressive messages against the idea. When a woman is ready for a relationship, she'll usually say something to the effect of "What are we?" If you aren't hearing those words, then there's a good chance she's not ready for a relationship. If a woman is ready for marriage, you'll usually hear something to the effect of "Is this going anywhere?" Proposing to a woman you haven't heard that from implies you're hoping the pressure of saying no is enough to make her say yes. Purple-pill, high-value men want to prolong the courtship as long as possible, although they're not opposed to a relationship. Purple-pill, high-value men just recognize a woman with all the qualities they desire, and rather than lose her once she starts throwing hints, they recognize it's time to shit or get off the pot. This is not a scarcity mind-set, by the way. It's only a scarcity mind-set if you get into a relationship with a woman you don't want because you're afraid of not being able to meet other women. As a purple-pill man, if you do everything right, you should expect a woman to want a commitment eventually. As a red-pill man, I expect it as well; the only difference is, I'm not really open to a relationship right now unless I'm completely blown away by a woman. Quite frankly, it would require a lot for a woman to blow me away mentally—so much so that I don't even think that a woman like this has been born. I just find the fact humorous of how things switch around so dramatically in the dating game.

CHAPTER

2

Getting Comfortable

Getting comfortable is a part of human nature. When you start a job, you usually get to work early initially and are very professional at the beginning. Let's fast-forward two years, and you're getting to work right before it's time to clock in, and that big, wide smile you once greeted everyone with in the morning is now a subdued head nod, if anything at all. You haven't gotten lazy or antisocial; you've gotten comfortable. This is an all-too-common occurrence in relationships. When you first met your girl, you had this sexy, charming, but serious demeanor that just lit your woman up on the inside. You were spontaneous and fun to be around. You had the perfect mix of masculinity and just enough of a soft side to have fun. Every evening with you was an "experience," and she couldn't wait to see you again. I'll discuss "the experience" in more detail later. Let's fast-forward a year, and that strong, sexy, masculine man she fell in love with is now nothing more than a playful, immature little brother. You can't even remember when the last time was the two of you had a fun evening out. A fun evening out isn't about predictably going to an expensive restaurant every Saturday night. Spending a ton of money doesn't mean you're having fun. You haven't stopped liking your woman, but you have gotten comfortable. You can never stop dating your woman. You were a man who had his purpose in life, but now you've thrown those plans by the wayside to spend more time with your woman. I know what you're thinking; isn't this what my woman wants? No. Correction: *hell no!* Women get bored easily, and this is a surefire way to ruin attraction. This doesn't mean you have to disappear for two months, but it also means you can't spend time with your woman every day. The perfect balance I've found that works to keep her off balance is to see her twice a week. Now I know some of you reading this book might be married or living with your girl, but the rules are the same. Although you live with your woman, I don't recommend spending more than two evenings together, with three being the absolute most. Winding down in bed before going to sleep doesn't count. I'm referring to getting off work and spending the rest of the evening with your woman. In other words, let's assume you get off work at five o'clock, and you're home by six o'clock. Let's then assume you start winding down for the night at ten o'clock and sleep by eleven. That would give you four hours to spend with your woman. If you're doing this, it's just a matter of time before she starts to pull back because she has gotten too accustomed to you. It's just a matter of time before she gets bored and starts lashing out from boredom. I can't speak for women, but I know for a fact that most men lose all of their identity in a relationship. When a man finds a woman he really likes, he drifts away from his friends, interests, hobbies, and purpose to spend more time with his woman. No woman wants to be the centerpiece of a man's life. Women think they want to be the centerpiece, but when you make them the centerpiece, they slowly lose interest in you. You want a woman to complain that the two of you don't spend enough time together. Now, if she's complaining because you go weeks without seeing her, then obviously this is too extreme. In dating, people tend to go to extremes with dating advice. The correct order should be purpose first, hobbies second, and the woman third. I put the woman ahead of friends because I'm not too keen on hanging with males that often. I think once a week with friends is enough. Never get too comfortable in a relationship and lose your identity. When I'm referencing a relationship, I'm speaking for rotation girls also. Although you might not be in a "monogamous" relationship, you are, however, in a "nonmonogamous" relationship. A nonmonogamous relationship is one that guarantees both parties, the man and the woman, will see each other regularly without a commitment.

3

Signs of a Quality Woman

The number one sign of a quality woman is a woman that's void of manipulation tactics. I'm at a point in my life when if I see any manipulation tactics being applied, I immediately lose attraction. A classic manipulation tactic is when a woman gives you full cooperation at the beginning only to pull back a week or two later. This causes men to chase not only the woman but also the cooperation she provided at the beginning of the courtship. Some women will even go as far as to sleep with you then pull back to get you chasing them. Signs of a quality woman are synonymous with a woman with high interest or a woman who views you as an alpha male, but not 100 percent completely. A woman could have a high interest at the beginning, which causes her to follow your program initially, but her female imperative to overly test your masculine core and confidence just gets the best of her. That brings me to my next sign of a quality woman: testing. If you're advanced, then you should know by now that women are going to test. The problem is that some women test way more than others despite you holding the masculine frame and confidence. These kinds of women aren't really trying to test your confidence—their top priority is to be as difficult as possible. Now you can say the being-difficult part in itself is a giant test, and it could be, but regardless of whether it is or not, you want to deal with women who keep testing to a minimum as long as you're not exhibiting signs of weakness. Some women pride themselves on being a handful. I think the phrase that's commonly used is "It takes a real man to handle me." I guess I'm not a real man because I don't need a woman whose sole purpose for living is testing her man on a constant basis.

We live in a different society from the one our grandparents lived in. This means that a woman no longer should depend on the man to pay for all the outings and bills if their relationship becomes something more serious. Initially, yes, but once you've engaged in a relationship or have developed a nonmonogamous relationship, there's no reason the woman shouldn't pay occasionally. If nothing else, it shows her appreciation for you. It doesn't even have to be a high-end restaurant, as the thought is what truly matters. If all she could afford was going out for wings, that would at least let you know she appreciates you. Some women genuinely believe the only thing they have to bring to a relationship is sexual companionship. A quality woman tries to bring other external attributes to the relationship. In fact, if you're a truly high-value man with options, you should almost demand that your woman brings something to the table. If she's financially unable to take you out, she'll just cook for you to show you her appreciation. Never put a woman in your rotation whose only attribute is sexual companionship. There's nothing wrong with casually dating these women, but it should be kept to that. The difference between a woman in your rotation and a woman you're casually dating is the regularity at which you see them. It's typical to see a woman in your rotation or relationship at least once a week. You should only see women you casually date whenever the opportunity presents itself.

CHAPTER

4

The Five Levels of Females' Interest

If you're reading this book, it stands to reason everything in your relationship isn't perfect, so I'm going to outline some common behavioral characteristics so you'll have a general idea of your woman's interest and you know where you stand. Most men think women are these complicated creatures that are hard to figure out, but in actuality, women tell or show everything you need to know if you're paying attention. Unfortunately, most men are delusional or in denial about a woman's actions. If a woman won't make a date, it's not because she's too busy. The president has time for things he wants to make time for, so what makes you think she's too busy to meet for a drink? Most men don't want to admit the truth about a woman's interest level, so they keep pursuing her, or for the guys who are in a relationship, they think just because she was head over heels in love two months ago that her feelings would never change. As humans, we fall in love, but we also fall out of love. My interest-level scale is going to go from five to ten, with ten being the highest interest level. If her interest is below a five, you should've left her a long time ago, because when a woman's interest is that low, she won't be a pleasure to be around.

An interest level of five is when a woman has a very low attraction to you physically. I say "physically" because, initially, that's all she has to go off of. Fortunately for us men, looks aren't as important as other attributes, like charisma and personality, so although you might not be able to light her fire physically, you can more than make up for it with your charisma. If a woman perceives you as a beta-male provider, her physical attraction or charisma really isn't a major factor. I used the term *major factor* for a reason, because you can't disgust her or be a weirdo to her. A *weirdo* is a man who lacks charisma toward that particular woman, although the better provider you are, the more lenient a woman's grading scales become. For instance, if a woman perceives you as a beta-male provider but you weigh four hundred pounds, and she doesn't find you that charismatic, $100,000 a year might not cut it for her to be with you. However, if you're that same guy but you make $2 million a year, all of a sudden your looks and charisma don't matter as much. For the record, unlike most dating coaches, I have no issue with a man using his success to get laid; I just don't recommend a man getting into a relationship, monogamous or nonmonogamous, with a woman who views him as a beta-male provider. The problem with trying to date women with this level of attraction is that you're far from a priority. Her attraction is so low that you're on the bottom of the totem pole as far as the other guys she's dating. This means you'll probably get the "We'll see" or "Can I get back to you?" when you try to set a date. It really just depends on what she has going on in her life. When you're that low on the attraction scale to her, she won't make plans with you if she has anything else going on. If you're a high-value male with a busy schedule, you should just put the ball in her court. Simply respond with "OK, let's just try to set a date when you know you're free." This simple takeaway might raise her interest slightly because it signals that you're not some desperate loser who's going to sit around and be her backup plan. This shows her you either have other options or that you have a backbone. Either one is extremely attractive. I want to make something emphatically clear: everything I state in this book is not meant to raise the interest of a woman but rather to help you be a man with principles and integrity. If it raises a woman's interest level, then good, but that's just a by-product. Everything a man does can't and shouldn't be about attracting women. If your only motivation for trying to obtain financial freedom or the body you desire is solely for attracting women, then you can never be a truly high-value male. Don't get me wrong—I want to look good for the ladies, so I don't want to act like it doesn't play some role in attracting the opposite sex. Richard Dawkins already has a theory called "the selfish gene," which states that everything a man does subconsciously is to attract women. While this may be true for most men, I can say for myself that women are just a by-product of my desire to achieve success and a healthy lifestyle. If a woman sees you as a five, maybe you can try to raise her interest with a short phone conversation or, better yet, a nice conversation when you meet her. Even doing that, your best bet is that she doesn't have much else going on in her social life. This low interest level also leaves you very vulnerable to flakes. The women who flake are usually selfish women who make plans with a man but who already know he's a backup plan. In other words, she made plans with you so she had something to do in the event her other plans didn't work out. When a woman says, "We'll see" or "I'll let you know," at least she's being courteous enough not to book a date when she knows you're not a priority to her at that point. While flaking is a sign of low interest, it's also a sign of narcissism and selfishness. I know women who are reading this are going to say, "Maybe something really came up," but I just find it odd that nothing ever seems to come up when a woman has a high interest in men when setting a date. In my experience, when a woman flakes due to legitimate reasons, she'll usually accommodate you that same day by either offering to meet later or earlier. She doesn't usually blow you off completely. If you're in a relationship and your woman's interest is this low, I can all but guarantee you she's "accepting applications again." Accepting applications is when a woman is mentally back on the market. I'm not really 100 percent certain that women are ever completely off the market, mainly due to hypergamy definitely not at this point. Just for the record, so I don't get arrested by "the ALL police," I'm not generalizing, as I know there are some faithful women in the world. There are always outliers to every rule; there are never any absolutes. I'm just going to speak from my perspective for a moment. From my experience, you can raise women's interest when you first meet them from their initial interest level, but once you're in an established relationship, monogamous or not, if her attraction drops, it's ten times harder to raise it back up. I have a theory for this, and I think it's the fact that once women see who you truly are, they aren't buying the change in level. Now is it completely impossible to raise a woman's interest back up after it dropped in a relationship? The answer is no, but it is much harder because she's formed an opinion of who you truly are. This is why sometimes it's better to start fresh. If you're in a long-term, committed relationship and your woman argues about everything, never wants to have sex, and gives you that look of disdain like she hates your guts, that relationship might be unrepairable. In a situation like this, it won't matter if you got back on your purpose or developed a masculine frame; she'll always see you as that weak, beta male. Just for the record, if a woman has a level interest of a five, she most definitely views you as a beta male at that very moment. Do not confuse a woman arguing and complaining about a lack of you two spending time together with a woman complaining about you leaving a dish in the sink as the same. In my opinion, it's a "good argument" when a woman is complaining about a lack of quality time compared to complaining about you leaving a dish in the sink. Her complaining about you leaving a dish in the sink is nitpicking and really isn't even about the dish but rather her building frustration and contempt for you as a man as a whole; her complaining for more of your time is actually a sign you're providing her the emotional motivation she needs to stay attracted to you. Women need something to complain about, so it can either be her complaining about a dish left in the sink or the lack of time you're giving her.

An interest level of six is better than a five, obviously, but only slightly better. A six won't get you laid or perhaps not even a kiss. The woman may give you a grandma-like, modest kiss, but it won't be a meaningful kiss. Truth be told, she's probably only on the date because she had nothing better to do. I guess that's not fair to say, considering it doesn't really matter what her interest in you is; if she had something better to do, then she wouldn't be on the date regardless. Women are very selfish with respect to a man's time. Most women are self-interested. I guess you shouldn't blame them, though, as their hypergamous nature instinctively dictates they take the best option for them at the time. Men largely aren't like this, as keeping one's word actually matters to a man. A woman could have an interest level of a nine in you, but if she happens to get an invite to Beyoncé's concert at the last second, she'll all of a sudden get hit with the stomach bug—a stomach bug called Beyoncé. I know you're thinking to yourself, why even go on the date to begin with if she has such low interest? Well, the answer is simple: as mentioned before, her interest level is mostly coming from her initial physical attraction level and your approach. You could easily raise her interest over the course of the date if you're confident and charming. Let's not forget compatibility. Men, the majority of the time, always find women compatible. That's not compatibility you're feeling; that's lust. Looks always will be what's most important to men, but women actually listen to the words that are coming out of your mouth during the date. To women, what you say matters. Things that don't really matter to men, much like interests and hobbies, really matter to a lot of women, especially if you're not drop-dead gorgeous to her. Of course, physical attraction conquers all as long as you're confident and don't blow it by running your mouth too much, but it's not often that a woman is going to be blown away by your physical appearance alone; therefore, what you say matters. No matter how confident you are, you have to be aware that sometimes a woman just won't like you. For us men, we don't look for compatibility in order to sleep with a woman, but if you're on a date with a woman who's looking for more than a one-night fling, compatibility is going to matter to her. She's smart and mature enough to know you won't be having sex 24/7, so she wants someone she can relate to. At this interest level, a woman won't initiate contact because, quite frankly, she doesn't care if she ever hears from you again. In this day and age, a woman won't initiate contact or pursue you at all because women these days are structured in that it really won't matter what her interest level is; she won't pursue you until she's somewhat attached. There are different levels of attachment obviously. I don't say that to be mean, but the facts are the facts, and if a woman has a low interest in a man, she simply won't put effort into making sure he doesn't forget about her. An interest level of six has a very high-risk flake rate also. When a woman has this kind of interest in a man, sometimes she'll flake for the simple reason of being a little tired from the day. That's right; she would rather watch reruns of *The Cosby Show* than spend time with you. You should expect that what might seem like a test is in actuality just low interest. That's another theory I think causes women to test men. I'm not quite sure it's testing at all but rather just genuine disinterest. I've been on blind dates before, and by "blind dates" I'm referring to online dating, because you never know who's going to show up. When women showed up looking very different from their pictures, I immediately became a sarcastic, disinterested person. This wasn't me testing the woman but rather just not being interested. The good news for a man is that women don't put nearly as much emphasis on looks as men do, so even if a woman initially has this disinterested look, you can quickly raise her interest with the right personality. The women who I met online who didn't look like their pictures didn't have this same option available, as there's nothing they could've said to raise my interest level. I don't think a woman starts testing until you raise her interest to a level where she's actually considering you as someone she might sleep with in the future. This could be to test your masculine strength, or it could be that, since her interest is so low, she doesn't care about offending you; it just all depends. That's right; when a woman's interest is on the low end, you're more likely to see her bitchy side. Understand that this doesn't just go for dating and trying to get to know a woman; it also goes for when you're already in a committed relationship. If you're in a committed relationship and your woman's interest level is this low, there's a good chance you're not having sex often, if at all. In my opinion—and understand this is just my opinion—once a relationship has reached this point, the relationship is over. Now the two of you might remain a couple for twenty more years, but that woman's soul left the relationship a long time ago. If she's the type to believe that a piece of a man is better than no man at all, then she'll stay. This would mean she's fallen into a scarcity mind-set during the relationship, which is common among couples. A lot of couples cringe at the mere thought of reentering the dating scene. The problem I have with this thought process is, how happily do you want to live your life? Do you merely want to exist through life, just happy to have someone to have dinner with and to sleep next to you at night, or do you want a mate who lights you up on the inside and who you have passionate sex with quite often? Don't confuse a woman being upset at you from time to time with low interest. No relationship is perfect, and there are going to be times when the two of you don't see eye to eye, just like when you and your friends aren't always on the same page. The difference is these rifts should be few and far between. If you're having rifts every week, then obviously you need to reevaluate the relationship. You may be able to raise her interest slightly, but I doubt you'll ever get it back to the point where she's head over heels with you again. If just having a mediocre love life is OK with you, then who am I to tell you differently? But for me, life's too short.

An interest level of seven is when you start to see some semblance of physical interaction with women. This physical attraction could be something as small as hand contact during a date. Trust me, it wasn't an accident. Women show their interest level if you're paying close enough attention or if you just know what to look for. Your flake rate is greatly diminished if a woman has this level of interest—but never gone completely. You can expect a kiss at the end of the night if you go for it as long as you did everything right on the date, and by "do everything right," I'm referring to raising her interest on the date. I advise men not to go for the kiss at the end of the first date, but that's just my preference, as I want the woman wondering if I liked her—unless *she* just goes for it. I've had that happen multiple times at the end of a first date. Unless you're uninterested, never refuse a woman's kiss if she goes for it first. Women don't handle rejection very well. I prefer to always ask a woman to come back to my place, as it's a man's responsibility to create an opportunity for sex. The goal should be to raise a woman's interest every date. In my opinion, if you didn't raise a woman's interest on a date, then it was a lost opportunity. The goal should be to raise a woman's interest to the point where she is comfortable sleeping with you. If you didn't do that, then you've wasted your time and money. A man should never enter a courtship with the mind-set of finding a girlfriend or wife. That's a turnoff to women, as it's a sign of desperation.

Women can smell when a man is actively seeking a relationship. If a woman entered the date with a level of interest of seven, then you should try to get it to an eight by the end of the date. The entire point of going on a date is to raise a woman's interest and get her more comfortable. Women have to feel comfortable with a man and have a high-enough interest before sex can happen. If you're a guy who meets a woman you like and you hope to make her your girl, you're going to have to raise her interest a little more before she starts thinking about a relationship—unless she's looking for a beta-male provider and you look like you could be a great provider. The only upside to a woman viewing you as a beta-male provider, if you want to call it that, is that you don't really have to raise her interest. All you have to do is look like you'll be a great provider, if that's what she's looking for. If you did a great job of raising her interest over the course of the date, then you probably stand a good chance of her coming back to your place. You have to think ahead about the logistics before going on the date. You have to anticipate your ability to raise her interest over the course of the date. Confident men always think they can raise a woman's interest during a date. But you may or may not have sex when you get back to your place. A lot of variables come into play when it comes to having sex with a woman for the first time. Is your place clean; do you have roommates who may show up any second; are you good at seduction, breaking down her last-minute resistance, and making her feel comfortable; is she on her menstrual cycle; and so on? I worked in sales as a trainer for a few years, and I can tell you that most people always have a last-minute objection or resistance, and it's your responsibility to overcome those objections and bring home the sale. Remember, most women will give you one last test before sleeping with you. That test usually comes in the form of testing your patience before sex. You have to let women get comfortable before engaging in sex with you for the first time.

Women want men to respect them, so this is an eternal battle that men know nothing about. Men don't have to worry about their reputations when engaging in sexual activities like women do. If you're in a relationship and your woman has an interest level of seven, you might have sex at least once a week. I do understand that sometimes the slowdown in the bedroom is due to the man not wanting sex very often because he's gotten bored sexually, but I'm coming from the premise that it's the woman who's not really in the mood often—and this is because I'm a male dating coach. I'm well aware that women get something from my content as well, but my primary audience is men, so keep that in mind when reading this book. If you're in a relationship, this is the interest level where things aren't all that bad—but they aren't all that great either. Things are kind of floating along without many problems. To be honest, this is where most prolonged, healthy relationships hover. By "healthy," I'm referring to not hating each other. It's just unrealistic to maintain that passion and intensity for extended periods of time unless you're one of the lucky ones who has met your soul mate. This is why we prefer not to get into extended, committed relationships. It's not that I'm afraid of getting hurt but rather the thought of just existing in a passionless relationship just for the sake of having someone. Most couples may have fallen in love at some point, but that's usually downgraded to just love after a few months or years. The difference between being *in love* and *just love* is that when you're in love with someone, you're still highly attracted to them as a whole. This is not just their physical being; their whole being gets you going inside, mentally and physically. When you just love someone, that means you just love them for the person they are, but they don't do anything for you spiritually. This is why a woman can love her male friend but not be *in love* with him. When you're in love with someone, their validation means everything to you. Couples don't remain *in love* all the time but stay together because they *love* each other. That's common because we all have expectations when we first meet someone. At some point, no matter how long it takes, the real us comes out. This "love" they feel has more of a friendly vibe than the "in love" passion they once had. This leads to the relationship feeling more like roommates than lovers. The key for men is to genuinely change from within. You can only pretend to be a high-value man for so long. When a man genuinely changes from within, there is no representative. You are the representative. When a man in a relationship is genuinely who he is, and if that's the guy she fell in love with, then it's impossible for the relationship to lose steam because there won't be any personality changes coming from the man. That doesn't mean the woman doesn't have a representative, but I firmly believe that men directly influence female behavior. When a man is confident and masculine, a woman can't help but stay feminine as long as her interest was genuine to begin with. I know there are women who are good at concealing their true intentions, but if you read this book, you'll learn the signs of interest from women.

An interest level of eight is when you start to become a priority to a woman. This is when you'll start to see a woman doing some of the pursuing—unless she's structured. If a woman isn't structured, she'll start to pursue to speed things along and progress the relationship. When a woman has this kind of interest, you start to see a very feminine woman. The best way to keep a woman in her feminine energy is to keep her interest level relatively high. When a woman has interest in this range, flaking is greatly diminished because there are not a lot of things she'll have a higher interest in. Expect a lot of physical contact, like holding hands or sitting overly close. Never pay attention to what a woman says or even does to a certain degree. A woman's body language is always the best way to gauge her interest. A lot of women know all the right things to say, and some even know all the right things to do, like cooking for you occasionally or giving you a back massage, but body language never lies. Women generally fake high interest with naive men who they perceive as beta males. Women's body language only displays this level of interest when it is high. She does this to feel your masculinity and to be reassured that you like her. A woman can only have this level of interest if she's uncertain of your interest level. I wish we lived in a world where we could tell women we loved them every day, but unfortunately women find this behavior boring and weak. The reason for that is you come across as uncertain as to where you stand with her. For example, the average person tells you they love you so they can hear it back. When a man does this, it comes across like he wants to make sure the woman says it back because he's uncertain if the woman still loves him or he wants to hear it to make himself feel better about where he stands with the woman. Women can intuitively read through this insecure behavior, and it's a turnoff. Anything that comes across as you being insecure starts to kill a woman's attraction. If you're in a marriage or monogamous relationship, I'm not saying you should never tell your woman you love her, but it should be done sparingly, as it makes you look insecure. A good rule of thumb that works for me when I used to be in monogamous relationships was to only say "I love you" in response to the woman if she said it first. Now you don't have to be that stringent, but you get my point. I know women are going to read that line and say that's a bunch of hogwash, but men with any significant amount of experience know that the women they had a low interest in always pursue them, but the women they had a high interest in flee more often than not. This is because when you have low interest in women, you do everything right as far as keeping their interest high because you really don't care that much. Keep in mind that the women you have low interest in will only pursue you if they have moderate or high interest in you. If she has low interest and you have low interest, she won't pursue you either. The point here is to always maintain the masculine frame and never let a woman know where she stands with you. When you get a woman's interest this high, it's obvious when it has dropped. When women's interest level drops, you start to see flaky, inconsistent behavior. She might start to flake on you, and her sweet, little early morning texts she used to send all of a sudden stop. When you try to set a date, all of a sudden it's harder for her to find the time. She used to always try to look sexy for you, but now she hardly puts any effort into her appearance. Now, this could be her getting comfortable, but more often than not, it's the fact that her interest level isn't where it should be for her to care enough to put in the effort to look her best for you. If you're in a relationship and you recognize your woman's interest level hovering around this point, then you're in a pretty good place. Understand that women's interest drops over a period of time, so this isn't a time to get comfortable. You could be in a good place today and be in a totally different place in just a couple of months. This is that "trap" interest level. This is when a man starts to let his guard down because his woman is usually making it easy for him by her use of limited tests and feminine behavior to the point he starts to lose his masculine frame. When a woman isn't as cooperative, it's easier to maintain the masculine frame because you know if you show any weakness, she'll walk all over you, but what if she's acting feminine? A lot of men take their foot off the pedal, so to speak, because she's cooperating.

An interest level of nine is when a woman has fallen in love with you. This is when you'll start to hear those three magic words: "what are we?" OK, in all seriousness, you might hear "I love you" also, but you can all but be assured that a woman wants to be exclusive by this point. If you're a guy who's not ready to settle down just yet, then a good reply would be "I like to take my time and not rush into anything." This will only buy you a little more time; however, most women are not going to let a man waste their time because women know their value to a man is mostly her appearance. So women who are looking to get married to the highest-value male they can attract aren't going to let a man take most of their prime years and then leave them when they've aged. If you're a guy who's just not the relationship type, you have to be cool with losing women from time to time. Some women will simply not let you use them for an extended period of time. When a woman is at this interest level, pretty much anything sexually you desire she would do, within reason. If you're a guy that's looking for a relationship, then this is what you want to hear. The funny thing about being a man who's looking for a relationship is you usually turn women off when you're looking for a relationship unless she's a woman looking for a relationship too. If you're a man who's looking for a relationship and you're dating a woman who's casually dating, it's very probable you'll turn her off because she'll be able to sense the relationship vibe you'll undoubtedly be sending. It's better, in my opinion, to be a man who's just enjoying the single life and to let love find you. When you're actively seeking love, essentially you feel incomplete and want a relationship to bring you happiness. In actuality, you should be content being single and have learned how to enjoy your life as a single man. A woman should complement your life, not be your source of happiness. This is why it's so important to have a purpose in life. If you're in a relationship and your woman has this level of interest, then just keep doing what you're doing, but if you notice a drop in interest, you need to get back to doing what you were doing. It's easy to tell when a woman has lost interest at this level. She won't be as enthused to see you as she once was. You might notice a slight drop in femininity. When women's interest level starts to drop, you'll notice a slight increase in bitchy behavior. You might also notice that all of a sudden, those freaky little things she once did in the bedroom have now all but gone. Women can only be 100 percent submissive to a man who's 100 percent in his masculine frame. This means you never put her ahead of your purpose and passion in life. The number one reason women start to lose interest, in my opinion, is men start to put their women on a pedestal. When a woman sees a man who's head over heels in love, she loses attraction because she now knows she's the one leading the relationship. It's OK for a man to love his woman, but I don't believe it's good when the man falls in love. It's hard for a man to stand up to his woman once he falls in love. Men always need to have the strength to walk away from a woman. This is virtually impossible to do once a man falls in love. This inability to walk away from a relationship is a big turnoff to women. It happens to be the only way to keep a woman submissive, because women have a tendency to cross the line from time to time.

An attraction level of ten is when a woman is basically attached to you. This is beyond a woman loving you; this is when she thinks about you 24/7. I don't believe women are capable of loving men for who they are. If a woman views you as an alpha male, I believe she loves you for how you make her feel, but if she views you as a beta-male provider, she loves you for what you can provide. I believe this because if a woman loved you for you, then it would be impossible for her to stop loving you. You are the same person, right? Well, what happened to her love? The answer is simple: you don't make her feel the way you used to. You probably got comfortable, and the relationship lost its intensity. It's extremely hard to maintain this attachment because we all tend to get comfortable, and therefore all the sexual tension you used to create by being indifferent you can no longer create since you've developed deeper feelings. A woman can only submit or stay submissive to a man who makes her chase his validation. This is, of course, if a woman perceives you as an alpha. It's impossible for a woman to become attached to a man she sees as a beta male. The reason I said "she sees" is that some women might view you as an alpha male, while others view you as a beta male. The only thing a woman is attached to with a beta male is his wallet. If a beta male loses his job and therefore can't provide as did before, he'll lose his woman if he doesn't get things turned around in a timely fashion. However, if a man a woman perceives as alpha—and who she's attached to—loses his job, the woman would stick it out as long as he made her feel the same way he always did. The problem here is that a lot of men get their alpha qualities from their financial situation and not their charisma; therefore, if they lose their jobs, they lose their swagger and confidence. This is why it's important to get your swagger internally rather than from external sources like money. A lot of men can have an abundance mind-set if they make a $1 million a year and drive a Mercedes G-Class, but if they lose their income, their confidence and indifference go away immediately. To be fair, every man feels better about themselves when they make more money, and I'm no different, but your confidence shouldn't completely come from something you have no control over. You can always lose a couple contracts or get fired. The woman became attached to you based on your confidence and the strength you exhibited throughout the relationship. You always led, and whenever she would test your masculinity by trying to take the lead or troll you to move you off-center, you were able to pass with flying colors because you weren't afraid of losing her because you felt you could replace her. You can't all of a sudden enter a scarcity mind-set and fear losing her. If a woman is with you because she perceives you as a beta male, then you don't have to worry about confidence; you just need to find another job quickly. When a woman is attached to you, she'll pursue you 100 percent. This, coincidentally, is the only way to keep her attached. So expect that from time to time she'll complain that you never initiate contact. Just hold firm and say, "I'm so busy I don't know if I'm going or coming most of the time." She'll still complain, but you should never initiate contact at this point. She's chasing your validation, and that gives you the power. This should only be done if your woman is attached. When a woman is chasing your validation, you don't have to worry about her pulling back. A female pullback happens when she loses attraction, usually because you're no longer a challenge or mystery to her. It could also be that the relationship has lost sexual tension and has taken on more of a friendly or roommate vibe. Another reason a woman pulls back is to strategically manipulate you into pursuing her more; therefore, she has the power in the relationship. The power in a relationship comes from whoever appears to care less. If you care more about her than she cares about you, then there is no way you could ever make her submissive. A woman is only submissive to a man she fears losing. A woman doesn't fear losing a man who loves her more than she loves him. Remember, she doesn't love you; she loves the way you make her feel. The way you make her feel is based on you having a higher value than she does, and that's why you don't initiate contact. You'll feel tempted to pursue her because your conscience will make you feel guilty about making her do 100 percent of the pursuing, but this is the best way to keep her chasing your validation. Most men think women want certainty, and therefore they try to do everything to alleviate this uncertainty, when in actuality women need this turmoil in their lives to maintain their attraction level. Why do you think women pursue the bad boy? The bad boy makes women feel alive. You don't need to ride a motorcycle and do drugs to give women this feeling. Just stay unpredictable and keep her chasing your validation. I also want to add that this is the highest interest level, and most men will never have a woman with an interest this high. A lot of men overestimate a woman's interest level. It's best to underestimate a woman's interest level; that way you never become complacent.

5

External Things That Lower Your Sexual Market Value

You must understand that anything that takes money out of your pocket lowers your sexual market value. Another thing you must understand is that this only pertains to women who view you as a potential beta-male provider. Women who view you as an alpha male don't care if you're homeless and unemployed. I can vouch from experience that if a woman views you as an alpha male, she won't mind you lacking in the financial department so long as you maintain your confidence and sexual intensity. That's where the problem lays. Most men who lack financial success, once they start to care about the woman or "catch feelings," let this lack start to create insecurities. I've had this happen in the past. Men are taught women love a man with money, and that's true, but this doesn't apply when a woman views you as an alpha male. So what exactly is alpha to women? Well, it's her perceived sexual market value of a man. If a woman thinks you have a high sexual market value, she'll deem you as alpha until proven otherwise. How does a woman determine your sexual market value? She does so based her physical attraction to you, combined with your swagger or apparent confidence. Generally speaking, unless you let yourself go physically, she's not going to lose attraction there. The point at which women lose interest is when a man loses his confidence.

A lack of confidence causes a man to act feminine—that is, unsure of himself. Women are very unsure of themselves; that's why they need constant male validation. Just so you know, acting insecure and unsure of yourself is a feminine trait. This state of insecurity you're in causes the woman to move into her masculine energy. Once this happens, the relationship is over. If a woman once viewed you as an alpha male but lost that attraction, she can never get back to that level of attraction again. It's sort of like your woman catching you cheating. She might not break up with you, but the trust is gone; therefore, her guard will forever stay up, causing her to never give herself to you completely again. The relationship, no matter how long it lasts, will never have that passion it once had because she'll be forever holding back. The same holds true for when a woman loses that alpha-male level of attraction. She'll never be completely 100 percent submissive because she now doubts your masculine core. You're as insecure as she is; how is she to trust you? Do not confuse confidence with arrogance. A lot of men make the mistake of trying to display confidence, which comes across to others as arrogance. What I've learned about arrogant people is that they are usually the most insecure. This is why they must remind you about how great they are. They really aren't trying to convince you, but rather themselves. Confidence is something that's just displayed— no words need to be spoken. Arrogance is when you verbally let others know of your greatness. Don't confuse this with trash-talking, as I was the biggest trash-talker in my video game and athletic days. I used to trash-talk to get inside of the head of my opponent. An arrogant man always crumbles once a woman starts to test. No matter how confident you seem, women will always test to see if it's what it seems. If you don't have a car, you have kids from a previous relationship, you live with your mother, and so on, yes, it does lower your sexual market value, but only to women who view you as a potential beta-male provider. The car and living situation are things that you can control, but you can't get rid of your child. This means that you've made yourself ineligible for a lot of women, but if you have an abundance mind-set, you should know there are a lot of women who won't mind. Even some women who view you as a potential beta-male provider might not even care as long as it doesn't negate your ability to provide. In other words, if you make $500,000 a year, a woman won't think you having one child will negate your ability to provide. However, if you have three kids and make $40,000 a year, she most certainly would, but who cares about dating women that view them as beta males? Don't get me wrong; I see nothing wrong with a man dating women who view him as a beta male, but I am damn sure not losing any sleep over the ones who don't want to date me because they don't think I'm a good-enough provider. I advise men to casually date women who view them as beta-male providers but to never get into a relationship or add these women to their rotations.

6

Some Women Will See You as Alpha, Some Will See You as Beta

In the dating community, there are primarily two categories men are put in. Those two categories are alpha males and beta males. Everyone wants to be an alpha male, although some men have no trouble telling you they're a beta male. How I classify an alpha male is a man who doesn't need to compensate women financially for their sexual companionship or time. Women will sleep with him with no monetary gain. When I say "monetary gain," I'm referring to gifts, cash, paying bills, expensive dates, and so on. I classify a beta male as a man who has to compensate women for their sexual companionship. If a woman views you as a beta male, but you don't have anything to provide financially, she'll just use you for attention and validation. This can be done with phone conversations or meaningless dates. Now here's the catch: you could have your finances in order even though you are a man she views as a beta male, and she still won't want to sleep with you despite her being open to being with a beta-male provider. Why is this? How could a woman be open to being with a man she views as a beta male but not want to be with a particular beta male?

Here's a simple example: Let's say you know that looks and charisma still play a small role in attraction even if the woman views you as a beta-male provider. You must understand that even if you don't mind being in a relationship with a woman who views you as a beta male, if she has another beta male trying to win her over and both of you make relatively the same amount of money, the deciding factor could come down to who she finds the most attractive. When I'm referring to the "most attractive," I'm not just talking about looks. I'm talking about the entire sex-appeal package. Some things I'm going to repeat in this book over and over, and that's so I don't sound like I'm contradicting myself. I want to make sure I'm clearly distinguishing one point from another. When dealing with women who perceive you as a beta male, you also need game, because women who are seeking beta-male providers are notorious for leading on men they view as beta males without ever sleeping with them. This is why it's important to keep the first few dates cheap and cut your losses after three dates. If a woman is seeking a beta-male provider, your financial situation is always the most important thing, as long as you meet her minimum attraction level. When I say "attraction," I'm talking about your sex appeal as a whole. That's looks, charisma, style, and personality. If a woman views you as a beta-male provider, as long as you meet her minimum attraction level, you don't have to raise her interest to sleep with her. She'll sleep with you out of obligation because you're providing. When I'm talking about women seeking beta-male providers, I'm talking about women seeking a relationship. Women obviously would prefer to meet a man they perceive as an alpha male who can provide. The issue with that notion is that those kinds of men are few and far between. Men who a woman views as alpha males aren't in short supply, but men who a woman views as alpha males who can provide and are open to the idea of being in a relationship are. A lot of the men women would view as alpha males are either in long-term marriages or not open to the idea of being in a relationship. This leads women who are actively seeking relationships to settle for the man she perceives as a beta male. I don't think it's a good idea for men to actively seek a relationship, but it's customary for a woman once she's ready to settle down to openly look for a relationship because she knows the clock is ticking. Her greatest asset, her looks, is diminishing every day. No matter whether a woman views you as an alpha male or beta male, most men will have to at least take a woman on one date or outing. This is usually because women need to feel comfortable with a man before she can sleep with him. This one date is also when she can figure you out to see whether you truly are as confident as you seem. I think most tests women do are largely due to low interest, but I do think women occasionally test to see if you are what you claim you to be. I say "outing" because it doesn't necessarily have to be a date in the sense of a dinner date or something of that nature. It could be something as simple as meeting for a drink. If she perceives you as an alpha male, she won't need many outings before she wants to sleep with you. Usually one will do, or maybe she needs none depending on her attraction level and her confidence in her sexuality, because a woman technically could've tested you when you met her—therefore, she doesn't need a date to test you. When I say "confidence in her sexuality," I'm referring to her ability to care less about what anyone else thinks of her sexual reputation. Most women don't want to be looked at as a whore or slut. Some women, however, in this new gynocentric society, *couldn't* care less what any man—or woman for that matter—thinks of them. I remember vividly in my early twenties a woman telling me that she just wanted to sleep with me. I can remember the shock I had, and my facial expression caused her to say, "A woman can sleep around just like a man. Why is it bad for me to just want sex, but not you?" This was my first experience with a woman who was completely comfortable with her sexuality, but it wasn't my last. And remember, a woman perceives you as an alpha male because whether you're considered an alpha male is totally up to the woman. Some women have been socially programmed to think guys who wear suits or preppy clothing are alpha males. Some women think that only bad boys—for example, gangbangers or drug dealers—are alpha males. I know this because I grew up in that type of environment, and those women didn't care about guys making the honor roll; they chased the guys who were in and out of juvenile hall. That fast life was attractive to them.

Another reason a woman would perceive you as alpha is if she sees you garnering a lot of female attention. This is usually due to some sort of social status. This social status could come from being popular, making a lot of money, being an athlete, and so on. This is called *preselection*. In my opinion, there's nothing that raises a woman's interest level higher than her seeing other women vying for your attention.

Last, a woman could perceive you as alpha just based on her attraction level. If a woman finds you very attractive, then she'll initially think that every woman must see you the same way. The only thing that can kill this kind of attraction is being insecure. An insecure man signals a man who's not very good with women. She then starts to doubt your sexual market value, causing her to test more and more. A woman testing an insecure man is like taking candy from a baby. There's no way an insecure man could ever pass these tests without first developing an abundance mind-set. I consider myself to be an alpha male, but I've dated women who I could tell considered me a beta male. The reason I think they felt this way is that physically, I wasn't exactly what they liked. Remember, with a woman, you don't have to be a ten in her eyes to get a date; you just need to be at least a five on a scale of one to ten. This low initial interest, however, will make her perceive you as a beta; therefore, you would need several dates to raise her interest. Upon meeting a man, a woman just assumes since you're not that attractive to her, you must not be that attractive to anyone, but you'll see a quick change in her interest level if she sees other women vying for your attention. If she notices other women vying for your attention, then she'll perceive you as an alpha male unless the women vying for your attention are only interested in your money or resources. If that's the case, she might consider you a trick and lose even more interest. Women do not respect tricks, or men whose game is so weak they have to buy women things for sexual companionship. Don't confuse a lack of respect with a lack of appreciation. A woman gladly appreciates a trick, but that doesn't mean she respects him. I have no problem dating women who perceive me as a beta male because I'm not looking for a relationship. Women tend to try to string along men they perceive as beta males much longer, so with this in mind, I advise any man to cut their losses after three or four dates—preferably after three. I only advise trying a fourth date if you were close on the third date. As a high-value man, you have to value your time and money. I know most men have been socially programmed to think they need to date a woman for two months before they sleep with her, but I can tell you from experience that same woman who's making you wait for sex has probably slept with multiple men on the first date. I know what you're thinking: is everything about sex? The answer is yes. See, the thing is a lot of women will use you if you let them. This could be for attention—for free dates with no intention of doing anything sexual with you. So you are not only wasting your time and money but also developing some feelings for her. This means that if you get the "I see you only as a friend" speech, it could leave you in a bad place mentally. She knew she only saw you as a friend initially but enjoyed the attention and free dates you gave her. This isn't about being afraid of love; this about being smart with your time and money. High-value men don't have time to date women who don't want them sexually.

7

Becoming a High-Value Male Doesn't Make You Immune to Games

A lot of men seem to have the mind-set that once they increase their income and lose some weight, all of a sudden women will start throwing themselves at them. This is the furthest thing from the truth. No matter how much money you make, women will always play manipulative games. This could be due to a lack of interest or just a woman's naturally manipulative ways. Men have to understand that being a high-value man isn't a state of being but rather a state of mind. In my first book, *Alpha Male Strategies: Dating in the Social Media Age*, I classified a high-value male as a man with limited time at his disposal. This means that he only has time to engage with women who have a genuine interest. In this book, I'll go a step further. A high-value man is not only a busy man with limited time at his disposal but also a man whose mind isn't preoccupied with women. The point is that, technically, a man could be busy, but that doesn't necessarily mean his mind isn't on women. You become a truly high-value man not only when you're not too available but also when your thoughts aren't consumed with females. You could be busy, but if you're wondering why that girl from the club never returned your call, then that isn't exactly acting like a high-value man in my book. A man has to also understand that he isn't the only high-value man in the world. For some reason, once a man gets a better-paying job, he starts to assume that he's the only man in the world with a high-paying job. The government didn't stop printing money once you got a better-paying job. Every day, several other men join the high-value male club. Getting your life in order doesn't make you God's gift to women. Getting your life in order just makes you a more attractive mate to a larger group of women. Women play games, which is why men get tired and settle down. Men don't settle down because they're tired of the caravan of women coming in and out of their bedroom, but rather because of the endless games that women play.

CHAPTER

8

Why Woman Make Beta Males Wait

f you're a man who's reading this who perceives himself as a beta male, you might've noticed it takes more work from you to sleep with a woman than it does to pass a law in Congress. Notice the phrase "perceives himself as a beta male." That's because if you're a man who perceives himself as a beta male, it's just the way you think of yourself. I don't think there are any true beta males. I believe some guys give up too easily in their pursuit of women. I get rejected by women, but it doesn't deter me from approaching more women (i.e., the abundance mind-set). Men who perceive themselves as beta males get rejected a couple of times, and they just designate themselves beta males who need to get rich for women to find them attractive (i.e., a scarcity mind-set). With that being said, the only difference between a man who perceives himself as an alpha male and one who perceives himself as a beta male is the abundance mind-set versus the scarcity mind-set. You see this in the business world; the alpha male has an abundance mind-set and starts his own business despite other businesses offering the same services. His abundance mind-set allows him to think that there's enough business to go around, while the man who perceives himself as a beta male always thinks that there are enough businesses offering whatever business he was considering, which means he's in a mind-set of scarcity. When I started my

YouTube channel, there were dozens of dating coaches already on YouTube, but my abundance mind-set allowed me to think that I could build my own audience. Men who perceive themselves as beta males let one rejection lower their confidence, but in actuality, had that same guy kept approached women, he would've met women who found him attractive. This is mainly because there isn't a universally good-looking or bad-looking guy in my opinion. I still can vividly remember when the "prison bae" (Jeremy Meeks) phenomenon was going on, some women said they didn't see what all the fuss was about despite a majority of women finding him attractive. I remember hearing this from female family members, who said this about Denzel Washington when I was a kid. Some thought Denzel was gorgeous, while others deemed him average at best. I won't lie to you and act like there isn't a general guideline for what beauty is and what it's not. I understand that the overwhelming majority of people would say Beyoncé is more attractive than Gabourey Sidibe (the woman who played Precious). I won't play on your intelligence and act like I don't know there's a general guideline for what's attractive. My point is, although an overwhelming majority of the people proclaim Beyoncé more attractive, there's always going to be some who find Gabourey Sidibe more attractive, no matter your opinion. I understand that if you put me up against Dwayne "The Rock" Johnson, I may lose if you took a poll asking women who's more attractive. I understand that, but what I also understand is that I'll get some who pick me. The reason I'm pointing this out is it doesn't matter if your friend or brother attracts more women than you. You're not in a contest. All you should be concerned with is attracting the women who find you attractive. So if you've relegated yourself to be a beta male, then it's your fault. With that being said, women make men they perceive as beta males wait for sex longer than they do men they perceive as alpha males. There are a few reasons women do this.

The first reason is obvious: low attraction level. Notice I didn't say "low physical attraction." That's because looks aren't the be-all and end-all with women as it is with men for the most part. If the woman is looking for a beta-male provider or a man she could build with, then she'll still date you because having fun with men she perceives as alpha males isn't at the top of her priorities at the moment. Don't get me wrong; she might have a "plaything" on the side, but for the most part, she's looking for something more stable. Understand that a woman's ultimate goal is to land an all-around alpha male and not just a sexual alpha. An all-around alpha has sex appeal and resources. The issue is that, although she wants to be with you because you're a man with his stuff together, she still doesn't find you very attractive; therefore, she'll make you wait because sexually you just don't do it for her. If it's the beginning stage of the relationship, there's always a possibility you could raise her interest to the point where she perceives you as alpha, but if it's already a prolonged relationship, there's a very good chance you'll never raise her interest to the point where she views you as an alpha male. Even if the two of you make it to the point of being in a monogamous relationship, she'll still have sex with you very sparingly. Expect her to have a lot of headaches during the relationship at night. You'll never experience the freaky sex men she perceives as alpha males receive. It takes a higher attraction level to receive oral sex and things of that nature. If a woman perceives you as a beta, she'll do the bare minimum. Women won't do any more than they have to, and without the woman's fear of loss, don't expect her to bend over backward to please you. The reason a woman views you as a beta male is she doesn't think you have a lot of viable options vying for your attention. This lack of competition causes the woman not to fear losing you, which in turn causes her to expend minimal effort throughout the relationship in order to keep you. Expect a lot of testing and masculine energy from your woman throughout the relationship due to her low attraction and respect levels. The low respect level stems from her constantly testing and from you constantly failing due to your scarcity mind-set. She'll get more and more bitchy, until maybe one day she can't tolerate your weak beta behavior anymore and leaves you because she sees you'll never have the balls to leave her.

Another reason a woman doesn't want to sleep with a man she perceives as a beta is that most men have been programmed to think that a quality woman doesn't sleep with a man within the first couple of months. The only reason a woman would date a man she perceives as a beta is to obtain a long-term relationship. She knows this won't happen if the man thinks she's easy, so she'll make him wait in the hope this makes him think she's a "good girl." Men who perceive themselves as beta males don't have a good understanding of the female nature and therefore don't understand the concept of high interest. Just because a man perceives himself as a beta male doesn't necessarily mean the woman would also perceive him this way, at least initially. A woman theoretically could find a man very attractive physically and deem him as an alpha male, only to find out he's really a beta male after a little conversation. Once a woman finds out a man has a beta mind-set, despite having what she would consider an alpha-male sex appeal, she knows she must make him wait in order for him to respect her if she's open to having a relationship with a man she perceives as a beta-male provider.

Last, beta males talk too much. Men who perceive themselves as betas are always trying to escape that title in their own minds and the public perception that they're a beta male. This leads the beta male to openly brag about his sexual escapades in the hopes he'll score social points with his peers and other women. I want to make something abundantly clear: women like to see you with other beautiful women; they don't like to hear about it in the form of your bragging. Although women try hard to screen this kind of man out, sometimes one will slip through the cracks. This minor slipup with the wrong kind of man could ruin a woman's reputation. As I've stated earlier, some women are comfortable with their sexuality and couldn't care less what anyone thinks, but the overwhelming majority of women still care about public perception. I know you're thinking to yourself, "I thought you said women don't sleep with beta males right away?" I would say that just proves my theory that there are no universally alpha or beta males. Some women will perceive you as a beta, while others may perceive you as alpha. This last scenario really only matters to women you interact with your everyday life. That could be a classmate, a coworker, a neighbor, and so on. If you're someone the woman doesn't see on an everyday basis, she might not care, hence why it's so easy to sleep with a woman when you're vacationing out of town or out of the country. I've always slept with random women when I went on vacation. This was due to high attraction, as well as the woman being freed from the social pressures of being labeled a slut. A lot of women think of a man in their neighborhood or job as off-limits, as it's too risky for them no matter how they perceive him. If you're trying to sleep with women you interact with on an everyday basis, and she is open to the idea of dating men she interacts with every day, the woman would likely just observe how you carry yourself from a distance. If you're a loudmouth, braggadocio type of guy, don't expect a lot of women in your everyday life to give you much play. However, if she observes you're a more laid-back type of individual and stay mostly to yourself, you'll stand a much better chance of attracting her attention. Women who don't have much to offer outside of the bedroom make men wait because they know sex is the only thing of value they have to offer. Don't expect a home-cooked meal anytime soon with these types of women. These kinds of women who have nothing to offer basically ransom sex for a commitment. You can usually spot these kinds of women on dates that really aren't that enjoyable intellectually and chemistry-wise.

Men Love Differently and for Different Reasons Than Women

M ost people have heard this saying before but may be unaware of what exactly it means. In a nutshell, men fall in love with a woman's beauty, and women fall in love with how a man makes her feel emotionally. I've had a lot of very nice women to whom I had a mediocre attraction level, and I was never able to fall in love with them. They weren't ugly by any means and could draw male attention, but they couldn't bring out that sexual passion from me as did some of the more attractive women I've dated. Keep in mind that looks are subjective, so I'm implying that they weren't sexy to me. Although some of the more attractive women may not have been as much fun to be with outside of the bedroom, I cared more about them because they were able to keep me sexually stimulated past the first couple of months. Now personality does matter, as I would rather have a woman I considered an eight on a scale of one to ten who I had amazing chemistry with as opposed to a woman I considered a ten but couldn't stand as a person. Keep in mind that a woman's cooperation is largely based on her interest and level of respect for you; in some ways the way you carry yourself has a direct effect on how a woman treats you, although you have very little control over her physical attraction to you. Just understand that although you may be dating a woman who acts like a brat, she won't act like that with every man she encounters. In other words, she knows who to play with. Most men think they're in love right now or think they have been in love in the past, but more often than not, they merely loved the woman as a person rather than being in love with her. I don't think men and women actually love one another. I think men love the "idea" of being in love or lust for a woman. That simply means an overwhelming majority of men love the thought of having a woman to call their own, or they simply lust for a woman they find highly attractive. Women fall "in love" with a man who makes them feel a certain way. A man who a woman perceives as a beta male could never make a woman feel this way, hence why women could never love men they perceive as beta males. Most men settle because they have a scarcity mindset and would rather be with a mediocre woman than continue being single until they find a woman they are highly attracted to. This is called settling. Being with a woman of this caliber does make it easier to pass her test, since your physical attraction is low, but you'll always have that feeling of something being missing. It's always easier to remain in your masculine frame when you're dating a woman you're not that attracted to, but this is why there are so many sexless relationships. Most people are with someone just to be with someone and basically in a relationship with their roommate. Men have to learn how to be alone rather than just settle for a mediocre woman, and by "mediocre," I'm referring to what's attractive to you. I'll keep repeating that throughout this book because I'm sick and tired of people thinking that there's a universal beauty. What's mediocre to one man might be beautiful to another man. The biggest issue I've found as a dating coach is this notion that some men consider themselves unattractive or uncharismatic. If I repeat it enough in this book, I hope to drive those thoughts out of the dating community. I bet if you were to think back right now about the woman you cared about the most or the woman you would get back together with if given the chance, she would probably be the most beautiful woman you've dated who had a tolerable personality. I said "tolerable" because I've dated some beautiful women who were mentally unstable. So I won't go as far as to say it's all looks—that would be unrealistic— but I'm willing to bet that dime you fell head over heels in love with was nowhere near the quality of that woman you considered a seven on a scale of one to ten who you dated even though she just did it for you sexually.

Women, however, fall in love through their ears because it's more about stimulating their emotions rather than their sex organs. Sex does play a role, but just understand that if you attract a woman mentally, the sex is automatically better because sex is mostly mental with women. You can get women head-over-heels crazy about you sexually without the mental stimulation, but you have a much better chance of pleasing her if you attracted her mentally. When I say "through their ears," most men think, "OK, I'll just tell her what she wants to hear." Unless you're dating a very young and immature woman, most women are aware of this tactic. Another thing to consider is that it doesn't matter if you say nice things to a woman until she has an attachment to you. Men need to learn balance in their dealings with women. The way to do this is with a strong, confident, masculine demeanor that she can respect but not so over the top that you don't know how to relax and have a good time. You can't compliment a woman too much to the point your compliments mean nothing, but you have to feed her a compliment from time to time. This should only be done when she's attached to you. If she's not attached, then you run the risk of lowering her attraction because you're giving her too much certainty. Ideally, I only like to compliment a woman if she's attached and asking for it. For instance, if she asks something to the effect of "Do you miss me?" then I would reply with "Of course daddy misses you." You must understand the only reason she is asking you that is you're such a mystery to her that she's trying to get some reassurance. Most guys go overboard with my "no validation" rule. While you don't want to give a woman validation initially, once you've built the attachment, you have to let her know you care sometimes. Keep in mind this book is largely about maintaining the attachment and not building the attachment. Her love will die if she thinks she's in love with herself. A woman wants a man who's not obsessed with her, but she doesn't want a heartless prick either. There has to be some balance with everything you do in life. The reason I don't believe you should compliment a woman until the attachment is built is, quite frankly, that it doesn't mean anything to her. A lot of men make the mistake of thinking a woman is going to like them because they constantly tell her, but in actuality the woman couldn't care less unless she's feeling the same way. In fact, this could have the opposite effect since you're basically being a butt kisser. Women are looking for a king and not a butt-kissing peasant. Constantly complimenting a woman is a sign she's of higher value than you are and is a big turnoff since she no longer has to wonder where she stands with you.

10

Women Know within a Few Seconds of Seeing You Whether They Want to Sleep with You

I f I had a dollar for every time I heard this chapter's title growing up, I would be a multimillionaire. I don't hear it as much today, but this false statement still permeates the dating world. It should be "Women know within a few seconds if they would be willing to sleep with you." The difference in the two statements is the first statement suggests women's decisions are based solely on physical attributes, like men's decisions for the most part. The latter statement suggests that while looks aren't everything to women, you do have to meet a certain level of attraction for women to ever sleep with you. This goes for men who perceive themselves as beta-male providers. Put in simpler terms, there's only a very select group of women who would sleep with a man who they have a very low physical attraction to for monetary gain. The overwhelming majority of women must find you somewhat attractive before ever sleeping with you. Keep in mind that looks are subjective, and there is no universal beauty. The latter statement also suggests that although the woman might find you physically attractive, you can still turn her off with your personality. Even if you approach a woman who was sending you choosing signals confidently, she still might not like you. The reasons for this could be from bad breath, missing teeth, being too corny, being too laid back, not being emotionally available, not being single, and so on. It really doesn't matter that the reason is; the only thing that matters is knowing that just because a woman is attracted to you doesn't mean you have your foot in the door. How many times have you gotten the number of a woman whom you felt had a high interest only to wonder why she is no longer willing to go out even though you know for a fact you were confident throughout the interaction? Compatibility matters to women and is something men rarely consider when dealing with women. The only scenario when compatibility isn't a factor is when the woman has a really high attraction level but is not looking for anything but casual sex. This is commonly referred to as a "sex buddy." Those women are very rare, however, as women get very little benefit from those kinds of relationships unless they have a man they perceive as a beta male who provides them with validation and dates. In that instance, a woman couldn't care less about compatibility and cares more about your bedroom skills.

The Experience

A lot of men want to know the secret to maintaining a woman's interest in the long term. For one, you have to keep dating your woman. When a woman is out on a date with her man, this date should feel like what I now call "the experience." "The experience" is not about spending an exuberant amount of money. The experience is more about sexual tension and seduction. A man has to have a woman when she's in her feminine energy to seduce her and create sexual tension. You can't seduce a woman when she's in her masculine energy. Keeping a woman in her feminine energy is solely based on her interest level at that very moment. Women don't have a high interest level in men they perceive as beta males; therefore, men who date women who view them as beta males can never seduce a woman. The sex is always something that seems more like a deal than a desire. It's typical for a woman to not willingly sleep with a man she views as a beta male unless he's constantly providing something. For starters, if you want to seduce a woman, make sure you're dating women who view you as an alpha male. Remember, every man is perceived as an alpha by somebody. If you are dating women who view you as an alpha male, just keep in mind that this isn't a lifetime achievement award. Just because she views you as an alpha today doesn't mean she's going to view you as an alpha tomorrow; it just boils down to her interest level on any given day. So first things first: you must make sure her interest level remains high at all times. If you're curious as to how to do this, check out my first book, *Alpha Male Strategies: Dating in the Social Media Age*, as I want to keep this book at the advanced level. Now that you have her interest level where it needs to be, you have to put some thought into the date. If you're a man of means, then there's nothing wrong with expensive dates as long as your finances are in order, but here interest level won't be solely based on how much money you're spending. I can tell you firsthand that my best dates of seduction weren't expensive at all. I won't go full-cheesy mode with the whole picnic-in-the-park ritual, but I can tell you a nice walk in the park around the lake while periodically stopping to make out on the benches while maintaining a seductive tone works wonders. Seduction has a lot to do with your tone, and when a man is unsure of himself, it's hard to have the right tone. This is why confidence is the cornerstone of everything dating related. When a man dates a woman who perceives him as a beta male, it's virtually impossible to have the right tone because a man who dates a woman who perceives him as a beta is always unsure of himself due to the lack of affection the woman gives him. A woman's interest level in a man has a direct effect on the man's confidence level when dealing with that particular woman. When a man senses a high level of interest from a woman, he naturally acts more confident, and when a woman doesn't have this interest level, he naturally acts more insecure. So what's the solution? The solution is to have an abundance mind-set and never settle for women who view you as a beta-male provider. I've dated several women who I could tell viewed me as a beta-male provider. The key is to never put these kinds of women in your rotation and most definitely to never get into a monogamous relationship with one. I simply just date them, and once the courtship has run its course, I keep it moving, as it's virtually impossible to raise every woman's level of interest to the point at which she views you as an alpha male. You will be able to raise some women's interest to that level, but not all. Like I've said before, just compatibility-wise, it's impossible to raise every woman's interest level that high, as there's a lot of variables in play. Looks, charisma, personality, and sex appeal are all subjective attributes; therefore, you won't be able to connect with some women on all levels. In other words, no matter what you do, you just don't do it for these women, so to speak. The problem is some men decide to get into relationships with these kinds of women, and the woman goes along with it because he could be a great provider, but the relationship will never have the passion that woman needs. When you're dating a woman and make the dates feel like an experience, you never have to worry about her losing interest. She'll be counting down the hours until she sees you again. This should be your goal whenever you're out with your girl or one of the women in your rotation. If you're wondering what the woman has to contribute to this experience, just keep in mind that she has a job to do also. If you're a high-value man with other options, then it's her responsibility to make you want to keep asking her out. So a woman's top priority is to be cooperative and feminine. When the woman is in the right energy, the man can take it from there, as a feminine woman is an easy woman to date. However, if she's acting masculine and bitchy, you're less likely to want to see her again. A woman can't fake her interest. She can try, but her body language always reveals the truth. A lot of her feminine energy has to do with how you're coming across, but some women get their masculine energy from outside sources, like work, friends, family, and associates. If you're dealing with a woman who doesn't know how to disassociate herself from outside forces when she's hanging with you, it might not be a good fit. We all have other things going on outside of our dating lives, but it's not your responsibility to have to deal with that and vice versa.

12

The Only Way to Gain a Woman's Respect

One of the biggest issues in a struggling relationship is usually the lack of respect the woman has for the man, besides the man dating women who perceive him to be a beta male to begin with. A lot of men don't understand how to make women submit or get women to respect them, so they resort to yelling and arguing with women. This only leads women to lose even more respect for them because these men are acting like women at that point. I know a lot of men don't want to hear this because most men live in a state of scarcity, but to gain a woman's utmost respect, you have to be willing to break up with her to gain that respect. The funny thing is, a lot of women want you to break up with them. Women can't maintain attraction without this feeling of strength on your part. Don't confuse a woman staying with you as an indicator of interest. When a woman is truly ready to leave a relationship, she'll usually try to push the man away by becoming an intolerable brat. She'll nag about any little thing in the hope the man will get tired of her. Unfortunately, most women still end up having to do the breaking up because some men have such a scarcity mind-set, there's nothing the woman could do to push them away. Once it gets this bad, it means her attraction level is so low that regaining her respect and love is out of the question. Without respect, there will be no love. That brings me to another point about being in a relationship with a woman who views you as a beta male: women don't respect men they perceive as beta males. I've never seen a woman be submissive to a man she perceives as a beta male. Whenever he suggests something that doesn't align with what she wants, she'll usually complain, and the man will usually comply. Women don't act like that with men they perceive as alpha males. They may test with the occasional pushback subconsciously just to see if he's maintaining his alpha state, but by and large they follow his program out of respect. If he's a man she perceives as alpha, she knows it's pointless anyway, as he never caves. This doesn't mean women can't have an opinion, but don't confuse having an opinion with not following your leadership. When the subject of which restaurant the two of you should go to comes up, she can voice her opinion, but ultimately, it's you who decides. When a woman is with a man who she perceives as a beta, this usually gets him the silent treatment and the cold shoulder for the rest of the night. This is because women know how easily men they perceive as beta males can be manipulated, which is why women don't respect these men to begin with. If a woman has become unbearable, the best thing you can do is save the little dignity you have left and break it off. At this point it's not even about gaining her respect but rather maintaining your sanity, as some women simply become flat-out witches. You can prevent it from getting that bad by simply ending things long before she becomes the world's biggest brat. Once you've noticed your woman not responding to your feedback about her bad behavior, you simply break things off. Despite what counselors may tell you, talks and lectures really don't work with women anyway. Women always respond to actions better than they do to words. If me saying this frightens you, then you know why you're having issues with your woman's bad behavior. When you break things off, you have to have to be prepared to never hear from her again. You have to be cool with that. If she was being a brat so you would end things, then it's highly likely you'll never hear from her again. However, if you showed the ability to walk away before her attraction got too low, then it's highly likely you'll hear from her again. Understand that you don't break up or leave a woman with the intention of raising her interest. You leave her because you enjoy your alone time more than you enjoy her. If she reaches back out to you, you should inform her that you didn't like her attitude at the end of the relationship and ask her how's she willing to make it up to you. This could be anything you want: sex, cleaning, cooking, and so on. It really doesn't matter what it is, as long as she is doing something. The reason for this is you don't want a woman to feel like she can just come in and out of your life whenever she wants. Maybe the reason for her behavior at the end of the relationship had nothing to do with you per se and was rather due to her having eyes for a new male coworker, so she wanted to date him and see where things could go, or maybe she was dating him toward the end of your relationship so she became an intolerable brat toward you—who knows? All I do know is that it sets a bad precedent if you just take her back. It says to her, "Hey, anytime you want a break from me to date other guys, just become a brat again, and when you're tired of that, you can always just come back home where I'll be waiting with open arms." It also sends the message that you're not just happy to have her back. Under no circumstances are you to contact her first, or you will live to regret it. You'll be emasculated every chance she gets. She probably doesn't even want you back but figures she'll get a sick thrill out of emasculating you. Contacting her first definitely won't raise your sexual market value in her eyes, as you're acting like a man who couldn't do better. Imagine having an employee who worked for you but quit to find a better job, only to have them come back to you for a job. Would you give them a raise? No! You might even offer them less than they were making previously. That's pretty much what's going to happen to her respect level for you; it'll decrease.

13

Why Choosing Signals Is for Advanced Men Only

When someone thinks of Alpha Male Strategies, the first things they think of are the masculine frame, purpose, offering no validation, and waiting for choosing signals. While most individuals understand my concept of holding a masculine frame, having your purpose, and offering no validation, most individuals misunderstand my concept of waiting for choosing signals. I want to clear up any misconceptions anyone might have as far as my philosophy with choosing signals is concerned. Waiting for choosing signals is not about attracting the most women. On the contrary, cold approaching women is a far better way to get more women's numbers. Anybody with half a brain can understand that a man who randomly approaches multiple women a day is going to attract more women than a man who doesn't. Choosing signals is about not basing your life around women and sex 24/7. Most men are in such a thirsty state that they can't even go out with friends and enjoy their friends' company without obsessing over women. The funny thing is, we live in a society where most men *claim* to have gone their own way, yet they can't even go out and enjoy themselves without women being the focal point of the evening. When you go to a club, you see women out just enjoying their girlfriends' company. Now I want you to look at the men in the same club; what are all of them doing? Most of the men will be looking at and obsessing over the women. Choosing signals is about being able to go on vacation and not needing female company to enjoy yourself. Choosing signals is not anti-cold approaching women or going into monk mode; choosing signals is about not letting your little head control your life 24/7. If you leave the house with the idea of going to the mall to buy a shirt but just so happen to see a woman you find attractive, then by all means, go ahead and cold approach. I just don't want you to leave the house with the mind-set of getting as many numbers as possible that particular day. If you leave the house with that mind-set, you'll always be in a state of frustration because your life is based on female validation. Telling men to never cold approach would contradict everything I teach because I firmly believe a woman's attraction to a man isn't fully just physical but rather to our other attributes as well. So a woman who views you as a five or six on a scale of one to ten might not necessarily send choosing signals despite her finding you somewhat attractive. Although her physical attraction is low, there's a probability you could raise her interest level with your personality. Telling men to only wait for choosing signals would basically be implying that men should stay away unless a woman has a high physical attraction. If you're a novice or beginner with no purpose in life and no women, then waiting for choosing signals is obviously not your best option, but novice or not, I still advise not leaving the house with the mind-set of seeking out women. In this instance, if you never get choosing signals, I advise you to look at improving your appearance, which is directly correlated to your confidence. This improved confidence is what gives you swagger. Swagger is how you carry yourself in a confident manner. This is a much better solution as opposed to spending all your time talking to women, hoping to get lucky. If you're a beginner and you're deciding to go to the club, just go with the mind-set that you're going to enjoy yourself. When I'm referencing being a beginner, I'm referring to not being very good with women or being a virgin. Age doesn't dictate whether you're a beginner, as some teenage men have more success than older men do. If you're out and just so happen to see a woman who may not necessarily see you, then go ahead and approach as long as it is a spur-of-the-moment thing and not a preplanned notion you had when you left the house. Waiting for choosing signals 100 percent of the time is for advanced, high-value men. This is because once you become a truly high-value man, you don't have time to date a woman with low physical attraction, because despite the fact that you could easily raise her interest level, over the course of a couple of dates, you simply don't have the time. Truly high-value men have the luxury of waiting for choosing signals 100 percent of the time because they usually already have women in their rotation and a packed business life. I'm not about to discard an evening with a woman in my rotation with a high attraction to date a woman with lukewarm attraction at best. I can remember back in high school when I had the opportunity to play basketball, I didn't want to play and practice due to my insatiable appetite to pursue women. Most men make money, but rather than investing the money, they buy liabilities—you guessed it—to impress women. A man's life can't be geared toward him getting laid 24/7. When you base your happiness on how many numbers you're getting or how many women you're sleeping with, you're always going to be depressed because no matter how many women you sleep with, no number is ever enough. When you base your happiness on pursuing your purpose and the kinds of hobbies you enjoy, your life will be so much happier. Let the women come to you and do activities you like to do. Most men are miserable because they do activities that they don't even enjoy for the sole purpose of meeting more women. This is why you see some men in the club who look like they want to commit suicide;

it's because they don't even like clubs, but they figure, "Hey, a lot of women are going to be here, so why not?" I'm not against the cold approach as long as it's organic. By "organic," I mean, for example, let's assume you're going to the supermarket to get some barbeque sauce, and you just so happen to see a woman you find attractive; by all means, go ahead and cold approach. What I am against is leaving the house to go to the mall for the sole purpose of meeting women. However, if you went to the mall to get the new Jordans that just came out, and you just so happen to see a beautiful woman in the food court, then by all means, go ahead and approach. It's all a matter of perspective. Now in a social setting like a club, I still wholeheartedly believe waiting for choosing signals is the best way to go. That's because in a social setting, a woman has plenty of time to observe you, and if she wants you, she'll let you know passively by flirting. While I think in a social setting this is the best way, I am not, however, completely against cold approaching as long as your intention when you left home was to just enjoy the event and not get numbers. I wouldn't do it, but I can understand if you wanted to do it. The reason I wouldn't do it has nothing to do with fear of rejection but rather the fact that it shows me she either has low interest or is not available. The lower interest is the more important point because it lets me know that physically, I'm not her cup of tea. As I said previously, looks are not the be-all and end-all with women, so I'm well aware I could raise her interest with my personality and charm, but when you become a truly high-value man, you don't have time to raise women's interest. This brings me back to the concept of the high-value man; if you're not a truly high-value man or working to become a high-value man with limited time at your disposal, you won't ever understand all of my concepts. Most of my concepts are based on being a high-value man. I know what you're thinking: if you don't have time to raise a woman's interest, why not just use a direct approach? Well, besides the direct approach just seeming highly inappropriate to me, I believe a woman will send choosing signals if she sees you as a seven, and definitely if she views you as an eight. That being said, I think a direct approach only works if a woman views you as a nine or a ten. I'm just opposed to raising a woman's interest from a five or six because you're so low on her priorities that there's a fifty-fifty chance that you'll ever get her to go on a date to begin with. If a woman views me as a seven and is sending choosing signals, then I know if I do everything I am supposed to on the date, I'm good.

How to Attract Women with a Busy Schedule

O nce you become a high-value man with limited time, one thing becomes apparently clear very quickly: you don't have as much time to go out with and meet women. While this is ideal for building yourself up and becoming a high-value man, it doesn't do much for your sex life. If you're a very busy man, one of the easiest ways to meet women is online dating. I can see you rolling your eyes at me as you read that statement, but hear me out. Online dating in itself is not the problem; the problem is that men let online dating become their sole way of meeting women. Men tend to walk right past an attractive woman on the street even if she's sending choosing signals, only to come home and respond to women online who only want online attention. In a way, online dating enables men, since it's much easier and less risky than approaching women in public. Online dating should be a tool but not your entire game plan for meeting women. When I use online dating, I only respond to women who have flirted with me online first and who I find attractive. This is kind of like waiting for choosing signals online. Once you become a high-value man, you don't have time to surf through hundreds of profiles anymore. That's a waste of time anyway, as a lot of the more attractive women by my standards who are online are either bots, only want validation, or get swamped by so many men they can't keep their names straight.

The next way you could meet women is by doing activities you actually enjoy. Listen, I'm all for men busting their behinds to accomplish their goals, but with that being said, you have to balance this with everything you do in life. What works for me is to bust my behind Monday through Thursday the entire day and then work minimally on Friday, Saturday, and Sunday. That allows me to go out Friday, Saturday, and Sunday evenings and enjoy myself. When I'm really grinding, it can be Monday through Friday working and enjoying myself on the weekends after doing only minimal work in the mornings. Now that's what works for me, but maybe working Monday through Friday the entire day and taking the entire weekend off works better for you. That's something you have to figure out. With that being said, it doesn't really matter how you organize your time, but just make sure whenever you do decide to enjoy yourself, you're doing something you actually enjoy rather than something that you think gives you a better chance of meeting women. If you enjoy shooting basketball in your spare time, I would be the first person to tell you it's highly unlikely you're going to meet women shooting basketball, but you'll have more fun shooting basketball than going to a club or social event if those things aren't something you enjoy. Another thing to consider is maybe you don't meet women shooting basketball, but rather you meet the woman of your dreams at the gas station on your way to shoot basketball. What's going to happen when you engage in activities you don't enjoy for the sake of meeting women is you're going to start pressing—you try so hard to meet women so you no longer have to go to that club or activity anymore because you don't actually enjoy the club scene or whatever activity you decided to do in the hope of meeting women. Now you probably won't meet women mountain biking, but maybe you meet the woman of your dreams on your way to the mountain. This is called the law of attraction, and I'm a big proponent of it. On top of that, you now have hobbies in addition to your purpose, which keeps you in an abundance mind-set. To maintain your abundance mind-set, you have to have hobbies on top of your purpose to relieve stress. You're now a complete high-value man who doesn't just depend on his purpose to occupy his time.

Last, men have to stop thinking they have to be dressed up to approach women. Listen, fellas; the best women you'll ever meet won't be at social gatherings, as most women go out to enjoy their friends' company or just to enjoy validation from men. A lot of women go out with their guard up, as they anticipate thirsty men approaching them all night. You stand a better chance of attracting a woman at the bus stop or grocery store when you're just going about your life. It's more organic and natural that way. Her guard is probably going to be down since she wasn't anticipating getting approached in the grocery store. Women are also humbler when they aren't dolled up with their sexy clothes and makeup on. As a high-value man, you have to learn to live your life on your terms and let the women come to you. This means pursuing your purpose, enjoying your hobbies, and meeting women organically along the way.

15

Still Getting Tested with a Masculine Frame

One thing that keeps coming up is that guys are surprised that, despite holding a masculine frame, their girl—or just people in general—still tests them. For the record, while holding a masculine frame does negate a lot of testing from others, it won't stop it 100 percent. You just have to understand that there are individuals who will naturally test more than others do. Some people just have the bully mentality. They actively seek out people who won't stand up for themselves. If you've had more than one relationship in your life, I'm sure you've noticed the difference in how some women test more than others do. A woman testing you directly correlates to her attraction level to you at any given moment. Just like a shark, if they smell blood, they attack. The same holds true for men. Some men are always in this childish bully mind-set, and unless you stand up to them, they'll only get worse. The thing is, there's a time to check them, and there's a time to ignore them. The same holds true for your woman. There's a difference between disrespect and trolling. If someone disrespects you, you have to check them. If a woman flat-out disrespects you, I suggest ending things right then and there. This is because women don't just disrespect you out of nowhere. It's a gradual buildup. You've been acting weak for a very long time, and now it has come to the point when she just flat-out disrespects you. Examples of flat-out disrespect are flirting in your face, staying out all night (if you live together), or just disappearing for a couple of hours after work when you can't get in contact with her. Quite frankly, a pullback isn't good enough if a woman disrespects you, because she'll get physical before long. You give some people an inch, and they'll take a mile. No man should ever hit a woman even if she hits him first, so to prevent being put in this predicament, I advise you to leave the relationship once you notice any disrespectful behavior. Don't confuse insecurities and jealousy with disrespect. You getting upset because your girl came home one minute later than she did the day before is insecurity on your part and not disrespect on hers. Your woman wanting to hang out with her girls for a friend's birthday is not her disrespecting you. If you feel insecure about things like that, then you're actually displaying to her that she's of higher value than you are, which causes her to lose attraction since women want men they can look up to. Women can't submit to men they perceive as having a lower value than they have. A woman trolling you could be something as simple as her mocking your bald spot, your three-minute sex sessions, or your lack of house-cleaning ability. If you notice this kind of trolling, then it's best to smile and keep moving or make a lighthearted joke in response. Under no circumstances are you to get angry and respond angrily. That's a sign of insecurity and only invites more trolling, or—even worse—she loses attraction. If you decide to respond with a lighthearted response, it should be done with a smile and with no malice intended. I believe in trolling back, but if you want to laugh it off and turn the other cheek, then you can do that also. Relationships aside, if another man disrespects you, you should always check him. In my experience, men have a propensity to take your nonresponse as weakness. The average man doesn't walk around testing other men, but there are some guys who are just naturally not good people and always looking for someone weaker to push around. The funny thing is, most of them are all talk, and if you stand up to them, more often than not they'll back down. Only cowards walk around looking for weaker individuals to bully. As you might be aware of, most cowards always back down when a confrontation is unfolding. Trolling, however, should be ignored, or you can troll back. The reason for this is there isn't any ill intent involved. They may even want to be friends with you. You can't expect to make friends if you're so insecure and sensitive that no one can even have a laugh with you.

16

How to Tell If a Woman Views You as a Beta Male

S ome guys aren't sure how their woman views them in the relationship. There is one surefire way to tell if your woman views you as an alpha male or as a beta male. When a woman views you as an alpha male, she will initiate sex quite often due to her attraction to you. This attraction could be anything from your physical appearance, to sex appeal, to charisma, to strength. When I mention "strength," I'm not referring to physical strength; I'm referring to your mental strength—in other words, your abundance mind-set. A man with an abundance mind-set can always check his woman when she tests his strength because of his abundance mind-set. Sex appeal can be considered a combination of physical appearance, charisma, strength, and swagger. When a woman perceives you as an alpha male, she'll naturally want to replicate your genes by way of sexual intercourse. When a woman views you as a beta male, you'll be the one having to initiate sex more often than not, if not all the time. This is due to the woman's low attraction level. When a woman views a man as a beta male, sex is more of an obligation than something she enjoys. I believe no man should get into a long-term, monogamous relationship with a woman who views him as a beta male. Remember, there are no universally alpha males; somewhere there is a woman who views you as an alpha male and desires you sexually. The problem is that most men settle due to their scarcity mind-set. If you're engaged in a long-term relationship with a woman who views you as a beta male, you'll never get to experience true love from your partner. Although I don't believe women love alpha men for themselves, but rather the way the men make them feel, it's still awesome to have a woman who hangs on to your every word as if you're the air in her lungs. When you date women who view you as a beta male, you'll never get to experience that, because women only love men they perceive as beta males for what they can provide as a beta male. This could be financial security, attention, relationship stability, certainty, and so on. If you've ever been with a woman who viewed you as an alpha male versus a woman who viewed you as a beta male, surely you could tell the difference.

Why Do Women Settle for Beta Males?

A lot of talk about women settling for beta males is centered around financial stability. While this may be true, I can make an argument that it's not the biggest reason. In my estimation, I think this lies with women actually maturing and wanting to start a family. At some point—for men and women—the game gets old. While most men already know that women enjoy their teenage years and early twenties with the bad boys, women usually gravitate toward the more stable guys—that is, men they perceive as beta males when they mature past that early stage. While the bad boy might have been fun in her early twenties, he's now considered an immature boy who won't grow up or commit—a liability of sorts. Ideally a woman would like to meet a man she perceives as an alpha male who's stable financially, and legally of course, and who has an abundance mind-set to check her, but this guy is extremely rare because even if she does find a man she perceives as an alpha male with all those attributes, he still has to be willing to settle down with her. See, that kind of alpha male usually has a lot of women throwing themselves at him, thus causing him to rarely want to settle down. This puts the woman in a conundrum: she can either keep waiting for a man she perceives as an alpha male to settle down or lower her standards in terms of her attraction level and settle for a man she perceives as a beta male. Although I'm cognizant of the conundrum the female is in, I still don't advise any man to get into a relationship with a woman who views him as a beta male. Only get into relationships with women who have high interest—that is, women who view you as an alpha male.

18

How Men with Nothing Attract Women

One thing that leaves a lot of men baffled is how men with nothing can seemingly attract beautiful women more easily than they can despite the fact that they have more financial success. Well, you must understand that although it may appear easier, this doesn't necessarily mean that it was easier. It could be something as simple as this man approaching more women than you did and playing the numbers game. If I'm shooting basketball and take a hundred shots at the goal, I'm surely going to get more baskets than the guy who only shot twice. While this may be effective in sleeping with more women, I still advise men to wait for choosing signals because my life doesn't revolve around sleeping with a million women. My life revolves around pursuing my passion and engaging in hobbies that I enjoy. In life you get what you put into it. The reason a lot of men aren't where they want to be financially is the same reason they attract more women than you do. Their life revolves around attracting as many women as possible. When I was a lowly paid security guard, I slept with a lot more women than I do now even though I make twenty times the pay. The reason for this is I simply put forth more energy toward sleeping with women than I did toward pursuing my purpose. Coincidentally, this is why I struggled financially for the majority of my life. You have to understand that your financial situation only matters to a woman once she's ready to settle down and start a family. When a woman is in the alpha-seeker stage, she doesn't care about your financial situation unless she just wants to use you. If you're wondering how to spot these women, it's easy. If a woman wants to use you for your resources, she'll be open to going on dates with you if it's somewhere nice but will play coy when it's time to show affection. If a woman wants to use you for attention, then she'll have all the time in the world to talk on the phone or text all day but always manages to have an excuse as to why she doesn't have time to go on a date. If she does go on a date, don't be surprised if she openly talks about other men who she's interested in. That's just her way of letting you know the two of you are platonic friends.

When they're broke and don't have much to offer in the way of finances, some men naturally increase their sexual charisma. However, some men lose all their swagger if they're not successful with their finances. Everybody is different. I for one lose a little swagger and confidence if my body fat gets too high. My financial situation has never influenced my confidence level. I guess you could say I've naturally never wanted to be liked for my money. Don't get me wrong; I like nice things, and if that attracts women, then fine, but I don't openly set out to attract women with my money. When I first started making money as a personal trainer in the city, I went out and purchased a nice vehicle. For the first time in my life, I tried to rely on my possessions rather than my personality. I quickly learned that leading with your wallet is a bad idea, as most women were turned off by me talking about my success. I quickly learned it was better to let my financial success be discovered than to openly discuss it. Some guys never lose swagger no matter what they do, but unfortunately every man isn't like that. Think of it like this: if you lose your sight, it's said that your other senses increase for survival. However, your other senses didn't really increase; they were always there, but you now are really using them since you have to for survival. This is why when men are incarcerated, they turn into poets, and that's for survival. A man who's broke can't rely on his success to get him in with women. Financial success can, in some situations, keep you from optimizing your sexual charisma. A man who's financially successful may have a propensity to rely too heavily on his financial success rather than his sexual charm. The biggest issue I have with other dating coaches is that just because they never lose confidence with women, they expect every man to have that same ability. This is simply not the case. It's a proven fact that more masculine men produce more pheromones, which makes you more attractive to women. Now I'm not saying every broke man produces more pheromones than successful men do, but some do. This is why the no-fap movement had such a huge following. I'm not here to debate whether not fapping increases pheromones, but what no one can debate is the fact that women are drawn to more masculine men.

The bad-boy effect is a real thing. Men who obey all the laws and never get into trouble don't understand women's fascination with the bad boy. The bad boy offers women an opportunity to escape their boring, monotonous lives and brings some excitement into them. Guys are rational, and therefore they don't understand that women are emotional and that consistency is unattractive to women. Women are small, frail creatures and since the beginning of time have always sought protection from big, strong men who offered it. Well, it just so happens that the bad boy offers most women this protective blanket they value so much. This is why it's so important to always stand your ground when a man tries to disrespect you in front of your girl. You don't stand a chance with her if she doesn't feel safe with you anymore. Any man who's ever had to stand up for their woman can attest to how much it turns them on.

A lot of men spend so much time trying to increase their financial success that they don't consider how important sex appeal is. Sex appeal is a combination of physical appearance, charisma, and confidence. A lot of broke men might lack the resources they would like to have, but don't have a shortage of sex appeal. Sex appeal is subjective, as looks and charisma are both subjective, meaning that every woman has a different taste as far as what's attractive and what's charismatic. What one woman may take as charisma may not be charisma to another woman.

Human beings have a herd mentality. You see this with a club or restaurant that everyone is raging about. You want to find out what the fuss is all about. You see this with television also; if you hear a show is popular, you'll be more inclined to give it a try. This is the same situation as when a man has a reputation as a ladies' man or is just popular with the ladies. Women just naturally want to know what is so good about this man. I've always said that a man's sexual market value isn't decided by how much money he has or how attractive he is but rather by how many high-quality, attractive women he can attract. This is called preselection, and it's why when you're single, nobody pays any attention to you, but the second you get a girl, it seems like every woman in town wants to sleep with you.

19

Charisma

From my general observations, I've noticed there are three different categories of charisma: You have sexual charisma, which is the kind of charisma that makes an individual a ladies' man. This is the smooth-talking individual who can charm the panties off any woman if he meets her minimum attraction level. There is no universally charming man. What one woman finds charming another might not. I think Kevin Hart is funny; you may not. That's because there isn't a universally funny person. It all boils down to taste. I think Steve Harvey is funny; you may not. I love *Game of Thrones*; you may not. There's nothing in this world that's liked by everyone. Some women love the charisma of a laid-back, smooth-talking man, while others prefer the joking, jovial type. So which one is more effective in attracting women? The answer is simple: whichever man lives more of a social life. You can be as smooth as Billy Dee Williams, but if you're going to live like a hermit, a lot of good it's going to do you. Men have to find the perfect balance between pursuing their purpose in life and having a social life. In my opinion, charisma, or lack thereof, isn't most men's problem; the problem with most men is that they are lazy and spend more time in their man cave rather than getting out and socializing. As the old saying goes, "No one is going to come knock on your door looking for you." As we age, we tend to live more and more on the inside. When we're young, we couldn't sit still for ten minutes, but as we age, the couch and a good football game become more and more satisfying. You have to force yourself out of the house on a regular basis if you want to have success with women. Just don't lose focus on your purpose in life—balance is key.

The next category of charisma is entertainment charisma. This would be the individual whose charisma has built them a large following because people like their personality. Take me, for instance; I have a large following via social media mainly due to my personality. There are tons of dating coaches on YouTube, but none get the views I get. The biggest reason for this is I'm just more likable than a lot of the other dating coaches. Dating-philosophy-wise, there are a lot of good dating coaches on YouTube, but they're boring. This is what's called the "it" factor. Now my personality on YouTube is a gift, and while I believe you can increase your charisma and confidence through self-improvement, by and large there's only so much you can do to improve your charisma. Look at it this way; you can only get so strong, you can only get so fast, and you can only get so much charisma. Our genetics cap everything we do in life. You can study as much as you want and read as many books as you want, but you'll likely never be as smart as Thomas Edison or Albert Einstein were. This shouldn't deter you, as there is no universally charismatic entertainer. Some people like my videos, while others don't. You'll never be able to please everybody. While I don't think there is a universally charismatic person, I do believe certain types of charisma are more liked than others. The same goes for looks. I think Beyoncé is attractive, but every man won't find her attractive; however, I think it's fair to say more men would find Beyoncé more attractive than Grace Jones. Although no one is charismatic to everyone, some personalities are liked more than others. So what's my point? The point is although I'm more popular than other dating coaches on YouTube, they still have their own following and are able to make a living doing what they love to do. The take-home message is that you shouldn't concern yourself with someone who is more liked by more individuals than you are; just appreciate the people who do like you for who you are.

The next category of charisma is friendship charisma. Some people just have an easier time making friends, while others struggle. Of the three, this is the one that I think can be improved upon the most, because I believe this is more about social skills—or lack thereof. If you're struggling to make friends, maybe you have an overbearing personality or are unreliable, untrustworthy, talkative, or not a good listener, to name a few things. The funny thing is, this could be an individual who's good with the ladies but struggles to make friends or vice versa. This form of charisma doesn't correlate with the others. Just because you can make a lot of friends doesn't mean you could build a large following. All three of these categories require a different skill set. As I've mentioned before, just because you aren't the kind of individual that can build a social circle of five hundred people shouldn't deter you from trying to make friends. Although someone else may have the personality to garner a thousand friends, in actuality a very small circle could be just as good. All you need is a couple of dependable friends you can count on. Don't let others' large social circles make you feel unwanted. Have an abundance mind-set, and just know you will be liked by someone.

How to Get Your Ex Back

I teach having an abundance mind-set, but let's assume for whatever reason your woman lost interest, and you really want her back. The only reason I believe a man should want his ex back is that he knows his screwing up caused her to lose interest. If you never stopped dating your woman, never got off your purpose, kept yourself in relatively good shape, and made sure the relationship kept its sexual chemistry, and she still lost interest, you shouldn't want her back. That's because she probably left you for another guy who she found more attractive or she just wanted something new. In my estimation, if she left you once for that reason, then what's to keep her from doing it again? However, if you let yourself go physically, lost your ambition in the relationship, and started showing insecurities, and after finding my work you now know what you did wrong and you've decided you want your woman back, then I think in this situation, it's justified since the loss of interest was your fault. Well, although you want her back, it's still her call. You can't reach out to her first because it shows you are desperate and lack confidence in your ability to find someone else better. You have to just move on with your life, and maybe over time, her interest level will go back up due to you showing strength and not pursuing her. If you don't pursue, there's a good chance she will reach out in a few weeks if she was ever attached to you at some point, despite losing that attachment. She'll probably reach out with what I call a "feeler" call. A "feeler" call is when a woman's curiosity has gotten the best of her, and she's curious as to what you've been up to these past few weeks or months. Understand that if you lost a woman's interest via acting weak and insecure, then you're not in a position to be demanding. In other words, I don't recommend you asking, "How are you willing to make this up to me?" because her interest is at a low point. Despite her reaching out, she's still in control. Asking a woman "How are you willing to make this up to me?" should be reserved for when you break up or pull back from her due to her bad behavior or when you know you were doing everything right and she still wanted out, probably due to another guy being in the picture. If she lost interest due to weak behavior, then technically she's in the power position despite reaching out to you first because her interest is so low that she probably couldn't care less about getting back with you at that particular moment. If you're lucky enough to get this "feeler" call, the best thing that can come out of your mouth is about how you've been bettering yourself because, believe me, she's going to ask. You might hear her ask, "So what have you been up to these last few weeks?" This is when you can let her know you're back on your grind. This isn't you trying to sell yourself as a beta-male provider but rather as a focused man who has found his ambition again. In other words, you've gotten your swagger back. Maybe you've decided to open that business you had been talking about so much. Maybe you've gotten back in the gym and lost that beer belly you gained during the relationship that caused her to lose sexual desire for you. In a relationship, ambition is highly important to a woman because of their hypergamous nature. Women need to see constant improvement. Even if a woman is with a man because he's a sexual alpha, at some point that thrill will wear off, and she'll want to see some ambition eventually. I think the phrase is "Love don't pay no bills." Ambition is a masculine trait, and a woman shouldn't have more ambition and drive than her man does. A content man is a single man. It doesn't matter if you make $5 million a year; a man should be trying to figure out how to make $10 million a year. A man who loses his purpose in life is a needy, insecure man who naturally turns a woman off. A man without a purpose is an available man, which is highly unattractive. What you don't want to happen is for her to reach out to find that nothing has changed. How is that supposed to help raise her interest? Women intuitively know that you'll be the same insecure man that you were before she left you. If she does reach out to you, you should by no means ask her out. There's a very good chance she's not there yet. If you do ask her out, she'll likely decline, and you have to start all over again. You should by no means call her. After the initial feeler call, it might take her a few more weeks to get back to the point where she wants to actually see you. You shouldn't be having two-hour phone calls either. She'll likely reach out sparingly every couple of weeks or so. You should keep the calls to no longer than five minutes before letting her know you're swamped with work. You're sending a signal that she's no longer the most important thing in your life; your purpose is. That's exactly what a woman subconsciously wants to hear. Hearing this lets her know she doesn't have the burden of being your entire life, which is too much of a burden for anyone, men included. By this time, the guy she's likely dating is starting to show insecurities and weakness. I know what you're thinking: I have to ask her out because it's unlikely she'll ask me out, right? This isn't just about getting your woman back. Trust me when I say you don't want a woman back when she has the power. You only should want her back if you have her complete respect, and she's following your program. I don't believe it's possible to raise a woman's interest back up much after it's dropped, but if you're just hell-bent on getting your woman back, I'm not here to judge. Your best bet is to get her to pursue you after a breakup. This is your best opportunity to reset the relationship. Women want a man who doesn't put them on a pedestal. The reason for this is men tend to gravitate more toward the woman and away from their purpose, causing her to lose interest. This could also be why she reached back out initially: she saw the signs the other man was putting her first again. A man with a purpose has no competition in dating due to the lack of other men with drive and ambition, especially once this man has found a woman he really likes and wants to spend time with. When she's at the point when she wants to see you, she'll say something to the effect of "Well, if you ever want to hang out, I'm off on Saturdays." Remember, although you want your ex back, you shouldn't be waiting for her. You should act as if she's gone and is never coming back. Only a small number of men are lucky enough to have a woman reach back out to them after they exhibit such weak behavior. Women are fickle creatures, and once they've left the relationship emotionally, they're gone for good.

Manipulation Is for Low-Value Men

I've been accused of being a master manipulator. If you have that interpretation of me, then you don't understand what I teach. First and foremost, I teach men how to become high-value men and how to value their time. Women will use you for free dates and validation; it's up to you to value your time and not let women who have no interest in you romantically waste your time. When I advise men to pull back, it's not to manipulate women; it's because you're so focused on your purpose in life that she gets less of your time, or her behavior warrants receiving more of your time. As a high-value man, you spend time doing the things you enjoy, and if her behavior isn't allowing you to enjoy her company as much as you used to, then you should pull back. That's only manipulation if you're doing it as a strategy. It just so happens to be what drives women crazy emotionally, but that's just a by-product of focusing on your purpose, not the sole reason. Remember, if you pull back, a woman only chases your validation if it means anything. If you're not striving to become a high-value man and instead have relegated yourself and are faking your value, then it's manipulation. See the difference? It's all a matter of perspective. If you resigned yourself to just pretending to be busy, you must understand that everything comes to light eventually. You can only fake your value for so long before the insecurities and neediness—which men who aren't focused on their purpose always have—show up eventually. You don't break up with a woman because you're trying to manipulate her into having higher interest. You break up with a woman because the value she's bringing to your life doesn't outweigh the negativity she brings. If you're just finding my work and you haven't discovered your purpose in life, I still advise showing high-value tendencies at the beginning, but this should be a Band-Aid, not a solution. The only thing that trying to fake your value for extended periods of time is going to do is have you meet the woman of your dreams only to lose her because of your insecurities. Becoming a truly high-value man is the only long-term solution. If you don't know how to become a truly high-value man, then I advise you to read my first book, *Alpha Male Strategies: Dating in the Social Media Age*.

22

Why Most Men Want a Relationship

I used to always get into relationships when I was younger. Perhaps the biggest reason for this was my inability to be alone. I didn't feel complete if I didn't have a girl who I could call my own. Looking back on it now, that's probably why I had so many different girlfriends in my twenties. If your main motivation for wanting a relationship is to avoid loneliness, then you're only going to lose that relationship. The reason for this is a woman should just be one aspect of your life and not your entire life. You should have hobbies, friends, and a purpose in life when she enters it. Another reason I always preferred to be in relationships when I was younger was the number of games women play. As I'm sure any single man can attest to, women, especially younger women, have an abundance of options, and therefore they're getting pulled in so many directions that they don't know if they're coming or going. Trying to maintain a young, beautiful woman's attention beyond two weeks can be daunting at times, causing men to get frustrated and to seek a steady relationship. When I was in my twenties, I didn't have a purpose or hobbies, and therefore female validation and companionship were all I would seek out. When you have a life you enjoy without women, this constant revolving door of women doesn't bother you because your life isn't dependent on female companionship. That's why, although I'm in my late thirties at the time of this writing, I don't get frustrated when women don't act accordingly. Women are a small, insignificant part of my life. Last, I'm well aware of men's great urge to start a family. If you're a purple-pill guy and you want to start a family, I can understand that. To be honest, most men who claim they're red pill today will ultimately go purple pill at some point in their lives. I'm not against men wanting families—or even a girlfriend, for that matter—as I've stated multiple times in regard to myself. I'm open to the possibility of getting in a relationship, but I'm so content and happy with my life that it would take one hell of a woman. So if you want to start a family, my only suggestion is to avoid marriage, as the laws don't benefit men in the event of the relationship not lasting. Most men think a prenuptial agreement protects them, but prenups aren't 100 percent foolproof, as family courts now void a lot of prenups if women can prove there were pressured into signing them. A lot of prenups also only protect the assets you accumulated before the marriage. Anything gained after marriage can be disputed. Maybe you're one of the lucky ones who maintains all of his assets after the marriage, but this is something that isn't worth the risk in my opinion. Women like the security marriage provides, so be prepared to hear ultimatums about marriage in the relationship. Also make sure the woman views you as an alpha male, not a beta male. When a woman views you as an alpha male, you'll get a lot more cooperation and a longer leash in hard times. Just make sure that if you decide to get into a relationship, you don't do it out of fear of loneliness. Loneliness isn't nearly as bad as getting into a toxic relationship.

Intuition

To me, having intuition is just another phrase for insecurity when it comes to relationships. Whether you're married or just in a long-term, monogamous relationship, there will be times when your intuition tells you something is not right. Maybe her daily pattern has changed, or she just doesn't seem as loving as she once did. While your intuition could be correct and she could be stepping out on you, my advice is to not say anything without proof. Discussing your suspicion with her prematurely is definitely an attraction killer. I don't advocate snooping or turning into a private investigator either. What I do advise is for you to get back to doing what you were doing in the beginning so you alleviate these assumptions. Women are methodical when it comes to planning, so it's highly unlikely you'll catch her in the act, even if she is cheating. More than likely, though, your assumptions are unfounded and completely in your mind. These assumptions say more about you than they do about her. Women cheat when they're with a man they perceive as a beta and not with a man they perceive as an alpha. The man she perceives as alpha creates sexual tension and turmoil; the man she perceives as a beta male simply can't duplicate this effect. While the man she perceives as a beta male provides financial stability, he doesn't provide the excitement that a man she's highly attracted to does. Keep in mind that attraction isn't just physical but rather the complete sex-appeal package, which is all the more reason why it's important for men to not get into monogamous relationships with women who view them as beta males. When you're in a relationship with a woman who views you as a beta male, you'll always have this intuition throughout the relationship. A woman could be with a man she perceives as an alpha male and still cheat because they're not connecting anymore. In other words, he's stopped dating his woman. Remember, dating isn't just going to nice restaurants; it's the entire "experience" of being with you. The fact you have so much time on your hands to calculate her schedule is a problem in itself. Women create space in the relationship due to an overbearing boyfriend or spouse. Women do change their patterns, but that's not necessarily to cheat but rather to create space because they're getting bored in the relationship. I won't deny the fact that men and women both cheat in relationships, but unless you have proof, confronting her just shows the woman you're afraid to lose her. My thinking goes as follows: If you can find a man better than me, I wish you and him the best. The reason I feel this way is I feel I'm a catch, and any woman lucky enough to date me should appreciate that. I more than welcome the competition. High-value men never think there's a better man out there than themselves; therefore, we never have these intuitive fears. High-value men are too busy pursuing their passions to worry about why their woman came home ten minutes later today. When a man isn't doing what he is supposed to do in the relationship, all these fears come into play. If you're having these intuitive fears, then I suggest you first look at your behavior. Remember, women need space, and if you don't provide it, they'll find it themselves. It's always better for you to do it because if she has to do it, then it means her attraction level is lower at the moment. This doesn't mean it's always going to be that way, but for the moment it is. You can provide the space either through pursuing your purpose or through hobbies you enjoy with friends. This allows her to miss you and never have a reason to create space. If she is cheating, then I believe everything in the dark comes to light eventually. This is another reason I believe a man should never get into a relationship with a woman who sees him as a beta, because I believe this increases the chances of a woman cheating on him. A man whom a woman perceives as a beta could never bring that lust and passion out of her the way a man she perceives as an alpha male can. Women need the stability the beta male can provide, but she also needs that passion a man she perceives as alpha can provide. Remember, it's all her perception; there is no universally alpha or beta male.

24

When Should You Never Take a Woman Back?

I teach men to leave women to gain a woman's respect. A lot of men might argue that you should never take a woman back. Their reasoning for this is that if it didn't go right the first time, what has changed? I counter that argument as follows: most women will subconsciously test to see if you have the strength to leave. Although I believe it's inevitable you have to leave women to show you have the strength to do so, there are situations when you should never take a woman back.

A couple of situations when you should never take a woman back are when a woman leaves you for another man, or you catch her cheating. The reason for this is it's probable she only wants you back because that relationship went south. If she did it once, she'll do it again. This shows you she's a cheater because she was dating that guy while she was still with you. Trust is very important to men, and if you can't trust her, you'll spend every available minute trying to keep tabs on her. If you're insecure because you're not following your purpose or engaging in hobbies you enjoy, that's one thing, but it's a different story if you're insecure because you have trust issues brought on by an untrustworthy partner. You'll never trust her again—and rightfully so. Loyalty is a trait that is either in you or not. Even if you exhibited weak behavior and she wanted a more masculine man, she should have ended things before dating anyone else. If you caught her cheating, who knows how long this went on?

Another situation when you should never take a woman back is when she is physically abusive. Society thinks it's funny when a woman hits a man, but I don't find it funny. Although women may not be as strong as men physically, nobody should put their hands on you. I advise men to walk away and not retaliate when hit by a woman. A woman hitting a man is a sign of the respect she has for you, and as we all know, nobody can love you without respecting you. I don't think it's possible to regain a woman's love and respect once it's gotten this low—if at all—so it does no good to walk away and then accept her back. It also shows the violent tendencies she has, because there are plenty of women who date or are in relationships with weak men who never resort to physical assault no matter how weak the man shows himself to be.

25

Breaking Down Male Nature

There's a ton of material discussing the many flaws of the female nature, but men rarely discuss the flaws of the male nature. First and foremost, men are controlled by their penises. It's been said that men think about sex every seven seconds. While I can't attest to the validity of that statement for every man, as far as I go, it sounds about right. When a woman is seeking a male to mate with, female nature dictates that she should seek the strongest genes and physical features. Society refers to these men as alpha males. I don't believe there are any universally alpha males, so I'll refer to them as men whom women perceive as alpha males. This is why it's imperative for a woman to test you. This testing allows her to know which category you go in. Just don't confuse a woman testing you with her just having a low interest. There's a distinct difference. We test women in a similar fashion subconsciously. When a man invites a woman over without having gone on a date, this allows him to know how easy the woman is subconsciously. Some men might refer to this as being direct, but as my momma used to say, people know who to play with. A man would never ask a strong, confident woman over to his place without having gone on a date first. If a woman accepts this offer, we might appreciate the high interest, but we usually respect the woman who makes us wait a date or two more. Although alpha males have a unique understanding of the female nature and don't usually judge women who casually sleep around, it's human nature to value anything you have to work for as opposed to something that's just given to you. A lot of women are taught this, and this is the primary reason women make men wait despite them having extremely high interest. This is commonly referred to as *social programming*. When a woman is ready to start a family, female nature dictates that she should seek the highest-value male she can to support the family. Society refers to these men as beta males. As I mentioned before, I don't think there is a universally beta male, so I'll refer to these men as men whom women perceive as beta males. Preferably, a woman would want an all-around alpha for this task, but she usually settles for a man she perceives as a beta-male provider. This is mainly due to the scarcity of men whom women perceive as all-around alpha. When that man can no longer provide, the woman will likely discard him and find a man who can. This doesn't happen overnight, as most women will allow the man time to get his life back on track—but the clock is ticking. Selfish as this may seem to men, it's the survival of the fittest. Women are hardwired to do what's in the best interest of their offspring or potential offspring. Notice that most of the female nature is centered around reproduction and providing for offspring. Coincidentally, that's what male nature is centered around. There are no ifs or buts about it; men want to get laid.

The biggest component of the male nature is our competitive nature toward other males. This is mostly due to the internal competition men go through to sleep with the hottest and fittest women. The reason we're drawn to hot and fit women is the same reason women are drawn to strong, confident, tall men. We instinctively want to reproduce healthy, good-looking kids. Notice I said "tall" men. That's because it's a fact that women "prefer" taller men, but don't confuse a "preference" with a necessity. I prefer a woman with double-D breasts, but that doesn't mean it's a necessity. The issue with a man's competitive nature is it can cause one of two things in a man. One thing it can cause is jealousy. The other thing it can cause is inspiration. A jealous man is akin to a hypergamous woman. They both can cause great harm. Men's testosterone level dictates a competitive nature with other males, but some men use this competitive nature to inspire them to perform greater deeds, while others use it to fuel their jealous rage. Men don't hate on men just for the sake of hating on other men. Men hate on other men because they're receiving the female attention they want to receive. I challenge all men to use that competitive nature to push them to strive for greater things as opposed to using it for destruction. I classify it as destruction because it's self-destructive. When you expend energy to hate on other men, it takes a lot of time and energy. You could have used that same energy for something productive, like pursuing your purpose in life. A lot of individuals would characterize jealousy as a female trait, and that statement may have some validity to it because we all know how feminized society has become. Men do have a lot of feminine characteristics. I, however, hold firm on my stance that jealousy comes from men's competitive nature. You see it also when women are competing for men's attention.

Ambition and drive are characteristics that every male should have. A lot of men lack ambition, and that directly correlates with why so many men have such a low sexual market value. Ambition is fueled by a man's insatiable appetite for sex. Most men would deny this fact, and that's because most men are unaware of what drives them subconsciously. Even if they're in a long-term relationship or marriage, every man subconsciously knows a lot of their worth to a woman is influenced by how they're able to provide—unless a woman perceives you as an alpha male. That perception is largely due to her interest level. Every man who's been in a relationship knows that sex dries up if financial hardships come about. This is because women lose all sexual desire when they're stressed about financial security. A lot of men lack ambition due to the society we live in today. We live in a society where everyone gets a trophy. Most men would rather spend time complaining about women's hypergamous nature or feeling sorry for themselves as opposed to improving themselves.

Last, men's nature is centered around an insane sex drive. While this is ideal for reproduction, this insane sex drive is what allows women to manipulate men with impunity. This insane sex drive is also what drives men to try pretty much any strategy to sleep with a woman. This is commonly referred to in the dating world as *game*. Most women recognize this at an early age and use it to their advantage. This allows women to strategically manipulate men for their time, resources, relationships, and even marriage. Understand that a woman isn't holding a gun to a man's head in order to receive these things. Men do it of their own free will in the hope of scoring points with the woman to ultimately sleep with her. This is why it's so important for a man to have a purpose in life. When a man has a purpose, it becomes a man's pastime, as opposed to chasing skirts. If left unchecked, a man would presumably spend all his free time pursuing women. Having purpose allows a man's big head to control his little head. Once a man has control of his little head, he is no longer able to be manipulated. This is because once you become a high-value male, you no longer tolerate low interest. You simply don't have time for it due to the amount of time you spend pursuing your purpose in life.

26

To Be Great, You Have to Sacrifice

A question I get hit with a lot is "How do I attract *a lot* of women while following my purpose?" I always reply with "You can't attract a lot of women while following your purpose." The reason I respond this way is if you want to attract a lot of women, you have to live a life of social abundance. So the correct question would be "How do I attract women while I'm on my purpose?" because *a lot* isn't plausible. A life of social abundance means you're out at least four or five evenings a week. As with everything in life, you get what you put into it. If you want to live a financially successful life with a thriving business, then you're going to have to put in the work. If you want to have a revolving door of women, then you have to put yourself in the position to meet these women by always being out and about—unless you're relying heavily upon dating apps, which means you're probably dating a lot of subpar women. My advice is, if you're a red-pill guy and want to live more of the nonmonogamous—that is, polygamous—lifestyle, you should sacrifice a for a little while to build yourself up before you become a full-bore womanizer. Just think for a second: wouldn't it be easier to juggle multiple women once you've made yourself successful financially? No matter how cheap you try to keep things, dating multiple women isn't cheap. Even if you're just getting drinks at happy hour, you'll quickly find out that dating multiple women can add up—not to mention that some women will only give men who appear to be successful the time of day. Wouldn't it be better to date a couple of women on the weekend for now and invest the other money you would spend dating other women? That way, your money is working for you passively later on. This is called *delayed gratification*. If you want to maximize your womanizing, then you want to make yourself attractive to these kinds of women as well. I'm not talking about gold diggers; I'm talking about the average woman who prefers a man with his stuff together. Quite frankly, I don't see anything wrong with that. The overwhelming majority of women you date aren't going to consider you an alpha male initially. You're not maximizing your potential if you don't want to sleep with women who perceive you as a beta male. Now, getting into a relationship with a woman who perceives you as a beta male is a totally different subject. Men are quick to get upset with women for wanting stability, but men are only attracted to a woman's beauty for the most part. I tell guys all the time that I had sex with more women when I was living in a basement with no car and making thirty grand a year in New York City than I do now driving an S550 Mercedes, living in a nice apartment in the city, and making over twenty times more than what I was making as a bouncer. How could that be? I just said money makes you more viable to more women. The thing is, if you're going to spend twenty-five hours of the day chasing women, then just by chance you're going to get some; it doesn't matter if you're homeless. The point I'm trying to make is that I left a lot of sex on the table because there were women who lost interest once they saw how I lived. There were some pretty hot ones who lost interest too, and it stung. The better approach would be to get your life in order first, then you don't lose women whom you have a good chance with because you live at home with your mom or you don't have a vehicle. There's no worse feeling in the world than to have a woman who finds you attractive but loses interest because you don't have anything going for yourself. Don't waste your early years chasing women; when you get to be my age, you'll regret it.

CHAPTER

27

Lying to Women Shows Insecurities

A lot of men have misinterpreted my lying-to-women method. If you're a man who's just finding my work and you're not following your purpose in life or living a social life of abundance, then I advocate lying to create value until you're busier. This should be a Band-Aid and not a lifestyle. It's much easier to just figure out your purpose than it is to constantly lie to create value. Being too available is a sign of low sexual market value, and the average woman loses interest. If you're a red-pill man and a woman asks you, "Are you looking or open to a relationship?" I advocate replying with "If the right woman comes along," and "I like to take my time and not rush into things." That's not a lie in my book, as every man, whether they know it or not, is open to a relationship if the right woman comes along, even if they're red pill. Red-pill men's standards are so high as to what an ideal woman is that it would admittedly take an extraordinary woman to entice them to settle down. That aside, men have taken my advice for lying to women to mean lying about every single thing they can. A good way to end up with busted windows and slashed tires is to lie about being monogamous when you aren't. Never commit to a woman just so you can get sex unless you're truly ready to be in a monogamous relationship. If you aren't ready for a relationship, just let her know that you're not in that place yet, and she either has the choice to keep seeing you or to move on. Lying about things like this causes way too many problems and headaches. In addition, some guys try to lie about their finances, and some short men even try to lie about something as silly as their height when using online dating. I'll be the first to admit using online dating as a tool to meet women should be kept to a minimum because women are pickier online, and one of the things they're very picky about is height. If you're short and decide to use online dating to meet women, you're at a tremendous disadvantage. Most women are going to disqualify you immediately. Be that as it may, you still shouldn't try to lie about this. For one, some women aren't attracted to short men. High-value, short men value their time and would never risk their valuable time by showing up to meet a woman who isn't attracted to short men. As a high-value man, you have to have the mind-set that your time is important and that you only want to give it to people who accept you for who you are. Additionally, this leads to a bigger point. Lying about your height shows a woman that you get rejected a lot and that your assumption as to why you're getting rejected is your height. It also points out your insecurity about your height. You have just subconsciously let a woman know you have a low sexual market value. Your height didn't give you the low sexual market value, but rather your insecurity about your height. Lying about your financial situation presents the same problems. A woman who wants a man with his stuff together isn't going to just take your word for it. Women who want men who already have their lives together are going to ask questions and observe you to determine if you truly have your life in order. As I've said, if you don't have your life together, a lot of women won't consider you to be a potential sexual partner in the same way some men won't consider an overweight woman to be a potential sexual partner. However, there are a lot of women who would be willing to work with you as long as they see you moving in the right direction. You don't want to waste your time dating women who aren't willing to work with you on your financial situation. Even if you meet a woman who's willing to work with you on your financial situation, she'll lose her attraction if she sees you exaggerating your financial situation. She'll assume that you must not be too successful with women and that you have resorted to lying about your financial situation as a way to attract them. Do yourself a favor and just let women know that you aren't where you want to be financially but that you're working hard to improve upon that. Either that's good enough, or it isn't.

28

Why Your Wife or Girlfriend Won't Have Sex with You

I've already addressed how to be better in the bedroom in my first book, but guys in extended relationships have been asking me how to get their woman to have sex more often. This is one of the pitfalls of being in a relationship with a woman who sees you as a beta male. Maybe initially she perceived you as an alpha, but as your feelings developed, you were no longer that strong, masculine guy who knew how to take control of any situation. Most guys can start off with the power in the relationship, but the woman slowly starts to run the relationship over time. The reason for this transition is quite simple: she's now your only source of sex. When a woman pouts early in the relationship, and the man doesn't cave, she later withholds sex as a means to get her way. If you cave, you must understand you're training your woman to withhold sex to have her way. When I was kid and would throw a tantrum, my mother didn't just let me have my way because she knew that would only encourage more inappropriate behavior. Technically, every woman in a relationship can control the relationship if the relationship is monogamous. Don't give me that crap about women wanting sex as much as men when we have eight to ten times the testosterone levels. Once you give a woman the power in the relationship by giving her a commitment, your only recourse is for her to know that not pleasing you is a cause for separation. Most men think that a woman not sleeping with them isn't grounds for breaking up, but I disagree with this assertion. When you give a woman a commitment, she's now solely responsible for keeping your needs met. She has to understand the two of you are not about to argue overnight about sex, and you damn sure aren't about to do her any favors in order for her to sleep with you. I know you're thinking to yourself, "Here he goes, telling us to leave our girls again," but men must have boundaries and deal breakers in relationships. It doesn't matter if the relationship is nonmonogamous or monogamous. Once you enter a monogamous relationship, it's very easy for a woman to manipulate the relationship by withholding sex. Let's assume the reason she is withholding sex isn't to manipulate the relationship, and let's then assume the answer isn't you not pleasing her. I would then suggest you try to have more risqué sex, like sex on the beach or sex in the park. If you're afraid of getting caught, then that's part of your problem. You need to spice things up. Show her you have a dangerous side. I for one get very bored of the same sex over and over, hence why I'm a noncommittal type of guy. Most people confuse my unwillingness to commit with me wanting to avoid heartbreak, but that's not true. The number one reason I don't commit is I know how quickly I get bored having sex with the same woman. Maybe you could go out dancing and screw her brains out in the bathroom—who knows? Just try to switch things up a little bit. She could just be bored. Remember that movie *Unfaithful* with Richard Gere? I know it's just a movie, but it has a lot of truth to it. You should be doing this anyway, but let's assume you haven't been; you could try having a life outside of her, like activities you enjoy so she can wonder about you. In this phase, she starts to wonder if you're seeing someone else, which creates just enough tension to light her fire again. This isn't manipulation; as a man, you have to cultivate a life outside of your woman. It just so happens this does manipulate her emotions, but that's not your problem. Honestly, though, I think spicing things up sexually should do it. If you decided to get into a relationship with a woman who perceives you as a beta male, then this is on you. You basically got into a relationship with a woman who has a low attraction to you. If you got into a relationship with a woman who perceived you as an alpha male and she doesn't want to sleep with you, it's because she no longer views you as an alpha male and has the same attraction to you as she would a man she now perceives as a beta. Women cannot submit to men they don't respect, and that's what a woman is doing when she sleeps with you. Another thing to consider if you're having this issue is your financial situation. When women are stressed about anything—particularly finances—their sex drive goes into the toilet.

29

Whoever Cares the Least Holds the Power

Most men have heard the age-old saying "The person who cares less has the most power," but how does one go about this? Of course, if you meet a woman you're very attracted to and who is very feminine, you're going to care about her. So what should you do? Well, a lot of men try to solve this problem by getting into relationships with less attractive women out of fear of not being able to maintain their emotional strength with a woman who really lights their fire. I don't advise men to get with less-than-stellar women to avoid losing their emotional center. The trick is to get the woman to care more about you than you care about her. You do this by constantly improving your sexual market value throughout the relationship. This should keep you in the abundance mind-set. You also have to maintain the sexual chemistry by not getting too comfortable in the relationship. If you want her to treat you like a brother, then act like her brother, but if you want to keep her feminine and submissive, you have to maintain a masculine sexual frame throughout the relationship. This is harder than it sounds, but it can be done with a little self-control. It doesn't matter if you're head over heels in love; as long as she values your validation enough to chase it, then you have the power. Once she starts to devalue your validation because you give it away so freely, then you have a problem. Remember, the biggest validation you can give a woman is your time. Once she knows she can see you anytime she wants, there's no need to chase your validation because you give it away so readily. I don't know how many times I've had to say this, but as a high-value man, you have to remain busy to keep your woman attracted. Working on your purpose feeds her hypergamous needs, and socializing with friends gives you social proof. If done correctly, your time with her will remain limited, which keeps her chasing your validation, which in turn gives you the power.

CHAPTER

30

Make Her Invest

One reason that men have a hard time keeping a woman attached is they fail to keep the woman invested in the relationship. The reason you want women to invest is it's human nature to stick things out once you've invested in a person or a project. Making a woman invest is all part of building and maintaining an attachment. This is why banks want you to put a down payment on a property or car loan. They know that if you start to have buyer's remorse, in a couple of months you'll be more inclined to stick it out if you've made a large down payment. Women's emotions change like the wind blows; one minute they're all over you, and the next they don't want to be anywhere near you. If you don't want your woman looking for the exit at every full moon, it's best to make her invest. There are three ways you can make a woman invest in a relationship, regardless of whether it's monogamous or nonmonogamous. You can make her invest emotionally, financially, and with her time. When you make women invest emotionally, essentially you're good at making her wonder about you. As I've mentioned, you do this by limiting your nonsexual attention and validation. You can make women invest financially by having her do something as simple as buying food to cook for you. If you live with a woman, I would advise you against paying all the bills. While you might think providing her with the freedom of not having to pay bills is what will keep her, it presents a bigger problem, and that problem is it prevents her from investing financially in the relationship. If you're well off and money isn't a problem, I still advise you against letting her avoid investing her money in the relationship, even if it's just a cable bill. As humans, we are emotionally tied to our money, since most of us have to trade our valuable time for it. This is why courts make you pay fines when jail time is not an option. They know you'll think twice about breaking the law when you have to pay money out of your pocket, no matter how small the fine. If you're in a cohabitation relationship or marriage, another reason I advise you against providing full financial support is that this is how you can easily be perceived by her as a beta male, which lowers her attraction—although she might be thankful for the support. She starts to think she has more value than you do, and you have to provide for her to compensate for your lack of sexual market value. The most effective way to get women to invest is with their time. I say this because, to me, time is the most valuable thing we have. This could be something as small as having her bring you lunch at work, stopping by the cleaners to pick up your clothes, or just bringing a bottle of wine over when she comes to visit. I typically make all my girls come see me. In New York, this could be a nice commute back and forth with traffic and all. I've had women tell me they wanted to leave me because I wouldn't commit, but they just couldn't go through with it. The reason they couldn't go through with it is I made them invest so heavily in the relationship.

CHAPTER

31

Imprint

An imprint is when someone makes such an impressive impression on you that you compare them to everyone you date thereafter. This is sort of like having an attachment that won't go away despite you not being with the person anymore. For men, more times than not, this is going to be a combination of the most beautiful and the most feminine woman they've ever dated. Remember, a woman's feminine energy increases with her attraction level. When a woman is being feminine, she's being very cooperative; therefore, you won't see a whole lot of testing unless you start acting weak. A man acting weak is a man who stops checking his woman and starts showing insecurities. There's no better feeling in the world than to be out with a cooperative woman with a high attraction level who is in her feminine energy. A woman's beauty alone won't leave an imprint because uncooperative women really aren't that fun to be with—not even sexually. They'll be barking out commands during sex. To leave this magical imprint on a woman, you'll usually need a combination of masculinity, confidence, sex appeal, and sexual market value. When you're with a woman, she observes how much attention she gets from you, and then she's able to calculate your sexual market value—unless she's already aware of your sexual market value before dating you. This usually happens when you date women you interact with every day, like at school or work. Outside of that, most women will do a background check of sorts. During this background check, she isn't looking for felonies or misdemeanors; she's asking around to find out if you've dated any of her friends or what caliber of women were you dating before her. You can't leave an imprint on a woman until you're the best she's ever had and vice versa. If you're able to leave this indelible imprint, it takes a lot to drop her attraction. You see this commonly with women who won't leave a man who's been caught cheating several times or won't stay employed. Once you've imprinted on a woman's mind, you have such a long rope to hang yourself with that it's virtually impossible to hang yourself. She'll stay with you for twenty years without a commitment, and even if she finally builds up the strength to leave, she'll usually reach back out in a couple of weeks to make up. In situations like this, it's usually the man who does the breaking up. There's nothing you can really do to leave an imprint on a woman but be yourself. It's more about compatibility than anything else. Every now and then, you meet a woman and you just do it for her in every way. From the way you look, to the way you talk, to the way you smell, you just hit everything right on the head. It's more about her taste than yours. Maybe you have just the right amount of humor and masculinity that she likes—who knows? If you're lucky enough to leave this imprint on a woman and have a fair amount of attraction to her as well, you're in an ideal situation to have your cake and eat it too. If you have a woman who's left an imprint on you, and you're no longer with her, that's not a good situation to be in. It could be ten years later, and you'll still be comparing every woman to her. Every woman after that point will pale in comparison to her. You'll find yourself reminiscing quite often about how hot she was and how you were able to have sex multiple times a day, but now you're lucky if the woman you have now is able to stimulate you once a week. My suggestion is, if you ever run into a woman who leaves the magical imprint on you, to make sure you remain in your masculine frame and keep her. The biggest issue with having a woman who's left an imprint on you is maintaining your frame. Although you're crazy about her, you always have to lead the relationship.

32

Choosing Signals Isn't a Guarantee

I teach men to wait for choosing signals. I teach men this so they can avoid being in a constantly thirsty state and not avoid rejection. Choosing signals do signal a woman's attraction to you; however, they don't guarantee you a phone number and a date. There are a host of reasons a woman could reject you even though she was sending you choosing signals. I know it's hard for some men to comprehend, but there are women who just get a sick thrill out of throwing out signs of high interest but really just want to lead men on. Some women will give you the indication of having genuine interest only to reject you. Some women will go even as far as to go on a date with you, give you every indication of interest known to man, only to ghost you later. When I was younger, we called these women "teases," but the phrase that's used today is "attention whore." These women value your validation and attention more than they value a man's money. You typically can spot these kinds of women right away because as soon as you approach, they go cold even though they were just giving you signs of interest. Sometimes a woman could find you attractive, but she's not available. When women see a man they find physically attractive, they might admire what they see, but if a woman is taken and her man is doing everything he's supposed to do, then you won't get far. I firmly believe that women only cheat if they're dating a beta-male provider or if a man they perceive as an alpha is losing his dominance and sexual charisma—unless she's just no good, which, if that's the case, you shouldn't have been in a relationship with her to begin with. If she's dating a man who's doing either of those two things, then I firmly believe most women start taking applications. "Taking applications" is when a woman starts giving out her phone number or taking phone numbers to find a replacement. This could be a tedious and long search that takes many months or even years. In some instances, a woman could just have a "plaything" on the side while she lets her beta-male provider do all the providing. I saw this for many years with female family members cheating on their spouses.

The approach you use is paramount in sealing the deal with women. Remember, when you approach a woman, more than likely she doesn't know your sexual market value, so the only thing she can judge it by is your approach. At the beginning, your sexual market value isn't determined by how you look, as looks are subjective; the confidence you display during your approach is how she gauges it. Women intuitively know what a confident man sounds or doesn't sound like. This intuition comes from years of being approached by males, kind of like how a detective is able to gauge if a suspect is lying to him. After years and years of interrogations, detectives able to pick up on certain body movements to know if someone is lying. When you approach a woman, your voice's pitch and body's movement let her know if you're used to dating women of her caliber. When you approach women who are not the typical quality of woman you date, nervousness will be written all over you. That's why it's paramount for a man to work on himself so he feels entitled to the quality of women he wants and this nervousness doesn't derail his approach.

You can't fake this confidence. Either you genuinely feel entitled to the woman, or you don't. I do think there is such a thing as having a poker face, where you can hide your nervousness, but it does have limitations. For instance, I think it's human nature to feel some kind of nervousness approaching a complete stranger, but there isn't a poker face in the world that can hide the fact that you're nervous because you feel like you'll be lucky to get a woman. Lines, to me, are corny. When I approach a woman, I just try to use whatever is transpiring around us to break the ice, so to speak. For example, let's assume a woman on a treadmill is sending me choosing signals, and I go over and approach. I would use the treadmill as a way to break the ice. I would say something to the effect of "You must be preparing for the Boston Marathon, the way you're over here running." That would typically put a light smile on her face, and then I would introduce myself. I always wait to see if the woman introduces herself as well as a sign of genuine interest. Women who aren't interested typically try to have a dry conversation to kill your advances. When I'm referring to a "dry conversation," I'm referring to her not contributing to the conversation by not asking you anything in return or giving very short answers. She does this purposefully, hoping you get the hint. The same way men have a game plan to attract women, women have a game plan to reject men as soon as possible if they have absolutely no interest.

Women are not like men in the respect that they don't value the importance of looks nearly as much as we do. With that being said, a woman could find you attractive physically, your approach could be confident, and she still rejects you due to your personality. As with everything else, personality and charisma are subjective as well. What one woman thinks is smooth and laid back, another woman may think is boring. What one woman refers to as having an outgoing personality, another woman refers to as immature. There are just different strokes for different folks. Some men like women who say very little, while I think these women are boring. Don't get offended if you're not a woman's cup of tea physically or personality-wise; just understand all you really need is one woman out of billions who genuinely likes you. Anything you're able to attract over that is simply a luxury.

CHAPTER

33

The World's Most Insecure Men

I think it's fair to say that the average person enjoys nice things. As men, we subconsciously know that wearing nice clothes, driving a nice car, and wearing jewelry such as Rolex watches are ways of showing women we can be good providers. Of course, there is also a fair share of men who don't have a pot to piss in and a window to throw it out of but who want to give off the illusion of having financial success. While using women's hypergamous nature against them is fair in my book, since women use our sexual desires against us to get validation, attention, and financial favors, the only women you're going to attract using your financial success are women who are actively looking for a provider. This is fine if you're looking for the occasional fling, but a lot of men then try to turn around and get into a committed relationship with these women. It's your life, and you're free to do what you want, but these women will never desire you the way you want them to. Another thing that a lot of men don't understand is that being excessively flashy is a sign of insecurity to a lot of women. When I was younger, the phrase I would commonly hear about men with nice cars is that the car was an extension of their penis, meaning that the car compensated for what they lacked in their pants. This same scenario plays out in women who dress like sluts and very promiscuously. There's a distinct difference between women who dress sexily and women who dress like sluts. When I see a woman who dresses like a slut, I know that's a woman with low self-esteem who needs constant male validation to make her feel better about herself. I feel this same way about men who need the big twenty-eight-inch rims, a Rolex, a diamond bracelet, and Gucci from head to toe. I mean, does it really take all that for you to attract a woman? I know, I know, you're wearing it for yourself—yeah, right. As with most things in life, there's a balance. You don't want to look like an insecure jackass wearing five designers at once, but you also don't want to look like you live on the street either. What I've learned is a nice button-down shirt, preferably custom made, or a polo-fitted shirt, if it's summertime, along with some nice fitted jeans and a good pair of designer shoes are enough. A nice watch and a ring are OK, but that's more than enough; if you need more than that, then it's probably safe to say you don't want that kind of woman these things attract around you. I teach men to not complain about the female nature, but rather to use it against them—and I stand by that—but spending all your money on dumb material items that depreciate is just silly and not something a truly high-value man does. Don't get me wrong; there's nothing wrong with having nice things, but you can wear outfits that cost $5,000, and it won't mean a hill of beans if the woman doesn't find you attractive or she is actively seeking a beta provider. You'll be much better off investing that money into something that'll create passive income, like index funds or real estate.

CHAPTER

34

How I Rate Women

Once you've become a high-value male with options, a woman's looks are no longer all she needs to get a roster spot or, if you're the monogamous type, a committed relationship. When you're a man with plenty of available time, you'll pretty much take anything that looks decent, hence why you struggle with keeping women cooperative. It's virtually impossible to keep women cooperative if you have such low requirements. Women can smell the desperation on you. I have a three-category rating scale I use to determine if a woman is worthy of being in my rotation. If you're the monogamous-relationship type, then you can use it to determine if a woman is girlfriend or wife material. The number one requirement is always looks. I wish I could say the number one category was personality, but I don't care what your personality is; if you can't turn me on sexually, it's a no go. The same holds true for women. Women do value confidence over everything, but you have to meet her minimum attraction level first before your confidence can come into play. If I had to choose between a dime with a horrible personality and a five with an amazing personality, I would gladly accept the dime. I would be miserable with a woman I wasn't attracted to. Of course, I would be miserable with the dime with a bad personality, but at least I would be happy sexually. Now, these are two extremes, and obviously I would prefer a woman I find highly attractive who has a great personality too. Thus, the next category would be personality. Personality for women encompasses feminine energy, which is largely based on her attraction level and interest. It does no good having a dime who views you as a beta male because she's going to exhibit low-interest behavior throughout the relationship. Compatibility also plays a role in this. If you're the ultraserious type, then obviously a woman who's a little bit more laid back and goofy might not work for you, although sometimes opposites attract. The next category would be responsibility. Responsibility is when a woman doesn't try to live outside her means via credit card debt, an expensive car payment, and so on. The reason this is important is if you decide to get into a relationship with her, she'll try to get you to do the same. You'll spend all your time working to pay for the overly extravagant lifestyle she wants. This will lead to stress and tension throughout the relationship, ultimately leading to a breakup in the end anyway, as finances are the biggest reason marriages and long-term relationships end. It's not the money itself; it's the stress the financial situation has put on the relationship to cause it to end. An irresponsible woman is the kind of woman who insists on going to that very expensive restaurant when the one you want to go to is just as good. You want women who have your best interests at heart. Ideally, I wouldn't put a woman in my rotation unless she has a combination of all three categories. Anything less than all three categories would deem a woman as someone I'm "just dating." The difference between a woman in my rotation and a woman I'm "just dating" is that women I'm just dating don't get birthday or Christmas gifts, and I'm not obligated to see them on a regular basis. This means I could literally disappear for a month before contacting them again if I so choose. I know what you're thinking: "What if they don't answer when I contact them again after such a long hiatus?" My response to that would be, if I actually cared, I wouldn't have disappeared so long to begin with. Women show low interest by not setting dates or using you as a backup plan, and men show low interest by not contacting a woman to set dates regularly or, if she contacts them first, they don't bring up getting together.

CHAPTER

35

Lack of Communication

I teach men to follow their purpose in life before and during the relationship. While doing this is going to keep you detached among other things, it's also going to cause the female to complain about a lack of communication between the two of you. Men in relationships think this is an issue, but this is what you need to keep women attracted to you. In my experience, women are going to complain about something because they're emotional and don't like it when things are too calm and predictable for too long—so they have to stir things up. So either she's going to complain about the lack of quality time you're giving her or she's going to complain about the dish you left in the sink last night, but one thing's for sure: she's going to complain about something. As a man who's following his purpose in life, this should be music to your ears. Besides the turmoil you're giving her to feed her emotional side, this is also a sign she actually wants to see you more. When women's attraction level drops or they view you as a beta male, they don't want to see you more; they want to see you less. When a woman views you as a beta-male provider, the more you work, the better. I can remember vividly my auntie preferring my uncle work as much as he could so he could provide more, and she could see him less. It seems to me that she preferred that he leave the house more and more. With all this being said, as with everything else, there's a balance. Most men go from one extreme to the other. Before they find my work, they go from texting their woman back within thirty seconds, texting back and forth all day, to expecting the woman to do 100 percent of the pursuing overnight without ever giving one compliment again ever. You can lower women's interest by overpursuing, but you can also lower it by underpursuing or just being a complete cold fish. If your woman is cooperating and acting feminine, then it's OK to throw your woman a compliment once every couple of weeks. First off, if you're not throwing around compliments every day, they actually start to mean something when you do give her one. Even if attachment has been built, she's pursuing you, and if she's complaining nonstop about a lack of communication, try initiating contact once a week. This shouldn't be a back-and-forth text session, but rather just a simple "Good morning. Have a productive day" should do the trick. A lot of the bickering about a lack of communication could be solved if the woman actually bought your story about being busy. My women never gripe that often because they can see all the things I'm doing; therefore, they don't bother me about my lack of communication, although I do get it from time to time. This is where being a fake, high-value male comes into play. I doubt you're working a full-time job and studying for the bar exam at night, and these women are complaining. The complaining comes from you saying you're busy, but to her, she doesn't see why you're so busy. Pretending to be a high-value male is only a Band-Aid and isn't meant to be a lifestyle because the truth always comes out.

36

Women Don't Handle Rejection Well

Once you become a high-value man, you learn to value your self-worth and lose your scarcity mind-set. This means that you no longer allow women to friend zone you in the hope that you one day become intimate with them. Don't expect women to take this well and just be content with you being cordial. I teach men to never show a woman they're butthurt about rejection—but don't play the lovable, gay male girlfriend either. In turn, you can expect women to take your cordial attitude and be dismissive toward you. By cordial, I mean you might simply say "Good morning, Melissa" and leave it at that, but since you're no longer pursuing and care to engage back and forth with a woman who doesn't see you in that light, now she's acting butthurt. Men have to value women's attention. You should never try to be friends with a woman you want sexually. All you're going to get is a case of blue balls on a consistent basis. The funny thing is, she knows you want her sexually but plays coy toward your advances to either keep you as a backup option or for the constant validation a beta-male orbiter gives her. The cold shoulder she gives you can rub you the wrong way, but you should expect it from women who have rejected you and whom you've decided to not let friend zone you as a way for them to get constant validation. Women compete with other women to see who can get the most beta-male orbiters. You see this on social media where women have millions of beta-male orbiters. Oddly enough, women don't give out free validation. If you go to some of the biggest male models' Instagram pages, you won't see a lot of women on them giving the men free validation. What you will see, however, is more men giving away more free validation. Men have to treat their validation like women treat theirs. Women do, however, give other women free validation online to boost other women's ego and self-esteem. This is one of the many downsides to dating women in your everyday living situations, like work and school. I prefer to approach and date women not in my everyday living situation. Even if she doesn't reject you, once the dating stops, this can create an awkward situation. The key word here is "prefer." I would prefer to date a woman in my everyday living situation, just like I prefer a woman with double-D breasts, but it's not a requirement. If you do decide to take this path, just be aware of the downsides to dating women in your everyday interactions.

37

Handling Women Who Seem to Have Lost Their Interest

As you might have guessed, I'm constantly evolving my approach to women. The higher value I become, the easier I expect it to be with women. Thus, I no longer ask women out during the initial phone conversation. I simply reach out and wait for them to initiate contact before I ask them out. This is a modification of my former approach of asking a woman out who has seemed to pull back. I changed this for a couple of reasons. The first is, as a high-value man, I don't want to waste my time dating women whose interest has dropped. You heard me correctly. Women will use you for free dates if you let them. What I've learned is that when a woman is genuinely interested, she will initiate contact even if it's just a simple "good morning." It doesn't take a whole lot of interest for a woman to accept a date for drinks. Understand that I'm fully aware that waiting for a woman to initiate contact after I've already initiated contact could cost me an opportunity with some women, but you have to understand that as a high-value man, my biggest asset is my time, not sleeping with women. This is one way that any high-value man can screen out women who aren't genuinely interested or who are losing interest. The difference between this approach and a direct approach, where sex is brought up rather quickly, is that I don't expect a woman to jump into the sack with me on the first date. All I want her to do is show genuine interest by contributing to the interaction. Another reason I've modified my approach is that I want to set the precedent from the get-go that I'm not trying to win a woman over; rather, we both should be trying to win each other over. When a woman is allowed to just sit back and let you do all the work, it can give her the sense she is of greater value. As a high-value man, you must understand what you bring to the table and send a signal that you're a prize too. Making her initiate after a drop in interest is also your way of making her invest.

Lack of a Social Life

Once you become a high-value male, you quickly find out that having a purpose in life can be a gift and a curse. It's a gift because it fills that void that we all have in life when we have too much free time on our hands. However, it also can put a damper on your social life. So what's the solution? I can't speak for everyone, but I don't grind for material items; I grind for financial freedom. I define "financial freedom" as making more money passively than my living expenses. For example, if my living expenses are $5,000, and I make $6,000 a month passively, that's enough to cover my monthly expenses and save something for a rainy day. If you grind to make money, but then you turn around and raise your living expenses to match your increase in income, you'll work until the day you die. I work a lot, but I look at it as a small price I'm willing to pay to achieve the elusive financial freedom most of us seek. If you have a demanding job, like truck driving that puts you on the road a lot, you might find it hard to maintain lasting relationships, monogamous or nonmonogamous. My advice for anyone in these situations is to make it as short term as possible and to save your money and either pursue another career or start your own business. Truck driving has a very high turnover rate, and that's for a reason. The same can be said for personal training. Jobs that prevent you from socializing for extended periods of time can lead to depression. We're social creatures, and a lack of socializing for extended periods of time can really impact you mentally. Life is for living and not slaving for eighty hours a week forever. I'm all for short-term sacrifice, but money and success just aren't that important enough to me for me not to live a life of social abundance unless it's temporary. If you're really grinding and don't have the energy to go out often in your spare time, then dating apps are probably going to be your best bet, despite all the pitfalls they have, because women can be extremely picky online. Some jobs are just not meant to be worked in the long term if you want to have a social and fulfilling life.

CHAPTER

39

Increasing Your Status

As men, we're unfortunately always going to have to deal with rejection. Following choosing signals and cold approaching attractive women are and will always be a numbers game for the average man, celebrities aside. With that being said, there's a host of reasons why a woman rejects a man. If it's a woman you truly want, there's only one way you can attract her after she's rejected you, unless the rejection was due to her already being involved in another relationship. In that scenario, she could've been interested but not available. Men need to understand that timing is always the biggest factor when it comes to rejection. That situation aside, the only way to gain a woman's attraction after that is to raise your status. There are three ways you can raise your status.

The first way to raise your status is to raise your sexual market value. This is when a woman sees you dating women of her caliber or better. This is commonly referred to as "preselection." Some men try to cheat the system and hang out with beautiful female friends as a way of trying to show they're preselected men. What men who try to do this don't understand is that women will send off signals to alpha males and other females to say that she's not with you. Women accomplish this feat with their body language. This will not only not accomplish your goal of raising your sexual market but also can actually cause you to lose sexual market value because it will come across to a woman that you're friend zoned, and therefore, if she didn't want you, then why should she? This is just another reason why men should not be friends with females they find attractive, besides getting the occasional case of blue balls. You're not just going to get up one day and start dating hotter women. This usually happens after you've done some self-improvement work, which improves your confidence, which then improves your success rate.

The next thing you can do is improve your social status. "Social status" is just another way of saying "more popular and liked." To me, this is the second biggest thing because it encompasses fame and popularity. The difference between social status and sexual market value is that social status is about being liked by men and women, while sexual market value is basically just being liked by more women. This is like the captain of the football or basketball team in school. Joining a fraternity helps in this area, as you improve your social circle. Most women are natural networkers, and it's very attractive to them when a man has a certain level of notoriety. If you're not an athlete, a fraternity is something you're not into, or maybe you're older, then you can always just try being more liked. To be liked by more people just basically boils down to fitting in with most social situations. Having a positive energy and not being a gossiper help greatly in this area. You have to be approachable as well. Try not to talk over people. A lot of men overdo it with the idea of the masculine frame and really make themselves unapproachable. There's a balance with everything; you don't want to be a cornball, but you don't want to be a scowling jackass either.

Last, improving your financial status is a great way to attract the woman of your dreams. Now I know a lot of men are going to say, "Hey, I don't want a woman to want me because I've improved my financial situation"—that is, they don't want to be perceived as beta males; I can understand that, but there's a big difference between a woman who wants shopping sprees and expensive vacations and one who just wants a man who has his stuff together. A woman could find you very attractive and view you as an alpha male, but if you live with your mother, she doesn't want to date you. In my opinion, there's nothing wrong with a woman who wants a man who has something going for himself, because quite frankly, I don't like women who have nothing going for themselves. If you think that it's stupid for women to want a man who is stable, then I guess we know why you're struggling with women. I made this the last item because while it does happen, typically making more money won't change a woman's mind unless it's a substantial amount. Be that as it may, it does happen. If my memory serves me correctly, I remember Steve Harvey saying something to the effect of his last wife telling him early in his career that he didn't make enough money for her, but after his career took off, she had a change of heart. So it does happen, but usually if a woman finds you attractive—and by attractive I'm referring to looks and personality—she'll give you a chance if she's available and sees that you are trying. On average, though, if a woman rejects you most of the time, improving your financial situation won't increase her attraction unless she just wants to use you or is looking for a beta-male provider, which means that she has low attraction. Dating women who are with you solely for financial reasons is definitely no fun, as you'll never feel missed or wanted.

40

Dating Women with Children

E very man would love the opportunity to date women who don't
have kids. If nothing else, it's an inconvenience to schedule dates
with women who have kids, considering the fact these women have
to find a babysitter if their children are underage. If they're older
kids, the woman might be involved in a lot of extracurricular school
activities. Also, there's always the possibility the woman might be
struggling if the kids' father isn't helping much financially. If this
is the case, the woman could be looking for a beta-male provider
to help her out financially with her kids. Oh, and let's not forget
the psychotic baby fathers out there who are still obsessed with
their baby mothers. These are always drawbacks to dating women
with children, but you're going to be missing out on a lot of good
women if you try to exclude women with kids from your dating
options. See, the fact of the matter is that the reason there are so
many women who are unhappily single is they exclude a lot of
men from their dating options. You have women who only want
men who are over six feet tall, have six-pack abs, and make six
figures a year, and then are baffled as to why they're single. I'm all
for everyone having standards, but some people get carried away
with their standards. A man should not date an unemployed single
mother with eight kids cohabitating with her babies' father—we
can agree on that. However, I see nothing wrong with dating a

single mother with two kids from a previous marriage who just so happens to be a lawyer with her own house. There is an upside to dating women with kids too. In my experience, they tend to never be needy because they are preoccupied with their kids in some kind of capacity or another. This might not work for men with no purpose in life, as they tend to have a lot of available time and prefer to spend that available time with women. One thing to keep in mind is that you can't be needy if you're going to date women with kids. Making a woman choose between you and her kids is the quickest way to find yourself on the outside looking in. Although I see nothing wrong with dating successful women with kids, for purple-pill men who are aware of the female nature but prefer relationships over dating multiple women, I would advise them against getting into relationships with women who have kids. This is the whole alpha-fucks, beta-bucks dynamic. The alpha-fucks, beta-bucks dynamic is when a woman has fun with the alpha male in her prime years only to settle for the beta to help raise the alpha's kids later on. I strongly disagree with men raising other men's kids. My advice is to date them but never wife them. If you're a purple-pill guy and want the whole family dynamic, then I suggest you date women with kids, but only get into a relationship with women who don't have kids.

41

Female Nature Misconceptions

Most men in the manosphere who are red-pill aware already know the ugly side to the female nature, such as hypergamy, chasing the alpha when they're young only to settle with the beta when they're older, and cheating on the beta with an alpha to replicate the alpha. Although this is primarily true, there are always loopholes in everything. I firmly believe in hypergamy, but I've seen situations where a woman would get hit on by men who have more money than the guy she was with does only to stay with the guy she was with. If it was only about the money, then why would she choose to stay with the guy who had less money? The answer is simple: confidence. Most men who have a very attractive woman usually start to get jealous and insecure when they know their girl gets a lot of attention, which in turn makes the guy start to lose his swagger once he develops an attachment. Some men, however, don't develop this insecurity, despite knowing their girl could attract a more financially successful man because, despite not having all the financial success of other men, he's confident in what he does have, which is his sex appeal. Let's not forget, now, that sex appeal is subjective. In other words, you have sex appeal if you believe you have sex appeal. There are some men who have six-pack abs, nice clothes, and a smooth voice and still lack sex appeal due to their lack of confidence, which is the cornerstone of sex appeal.

So it's not a look that gives you sex appeal; it's a mind-set that gives you sex appeal. Most men believe that due to the female nature, if they lose their job, their woman is going to leave them. Let's be honest here; if you lose your job and throw a pity party for yourself over the next six months, then, yes, your woman is going to leave you, but if you're the type of guy who doesn't lose his confidence and gets right back on the horse, I firmly believe a woman would stick it out as long as you made a relatively quick recovery. I also want to point out that this info is for alpha male–minded guys, as a beta male lacks the mind-set needed to maintain the masculine frame during hardships. Men who perceive themselves as beta males primarily rely on their financial success to attract women; therefore, it's virtually impossible for a man with a beta-male mind-set to maintain any semblance of attraction during a hardship. His confidence is tied to his financial success. A woman really doesn't care about a beta male anyway other than about what he can provide, so it's easy to see why women would leave these men during hardship, but if you read my first book, *Alpha Male Strategies: Dating in the Social Media Age*, then you should have developed the mind-set of a high-value man. Therefore, that shouldn't be an issue for you. If you're a high-value male with an abundance mind-set, then you should know women don't leave because you lost your job; they leave because you lost your confidence and swagger. Another big misconception is that all women cheat. While I do think it's possible for any woman to cheat, I wholeheartedly believe that as long as a man is maintaining frame and keeping the sexual passion in the relationship, a woman won't cheat. That being said, most men don't maintain frame and sexual passion throughout a monogamous relationship. Most men get complacent and lazy during a relationship. A lot of men bring their A game during courtship but bring their D game during a relationship. Women get bored easily, and even if their fond of the person you are, it might be worthwhile for you to try something new sexually from time to time. Most men can withstand a woman's test during the courtship only to fail it once they've developed an attachment. This weakening behavior will cause a woman to seek pleasure from a more dominant man. To be fair, while I think any woman is capable of cheating, some women do have integrity and would rather end things than cheat on you. Whether she cheats or leaves boils down to a couple of scenarios. If she's with you because she perceives you as a beta male and as a good provider, but she lacks integrity, then she'll cheat. If she's with you because she perceives you as an alpha male, but you lost your swagger and the relationship lost its passion, then she'll leave because your swagger was the only reason she was with you. If a woman is with you because she deemed you to be an alpha male, then you have no value to her if you lose your swagger; therefore, there is no reason to cheat. She might as well leave the relationship. If a woman is with you because she perceives you as a beta male, then she is always susceptible to cheating because, often, she isn't even attracted to you sexually but rather to what you can provide financially. Remember, attraction isn't just looks; it's your whole being as a man. If a woman perceives you as an alpha male, and you maintain your swagger throughout the relationship, I wholeheartedly doubt she would cheat on you because she'll be too busy chasing your validation to cheat.

CHAPTER

42

Let Her Come Back to You

There's going to come a time in every long-term relationship when there's either going to be a separation or a complete breakup altogether. If this is a woman you're basically tired of, then this won't be an issue for you, but when it's a woman you still care for tremendously, it can be heart wrenching. Your masculinity as a man will get tested. You're going to have some sleepless nights when you wonder if she has met another guy or, even worse, if she's sleeping with another guy. As a man, you can't control what she's doing during a breakup, but what you can control is what you're doing during a breakup. First off, you have to have the mind-set that she's gone and never coming back. You definitely can't call her first, as that would either cause her to lose all attraction due to your lack of strength or give her permission to emasculate you. Women expect men to have more strength than they do. She can know you're hurting, but it's something different when she knows you don't have enough strength as a man not to cave. On TV, you see men coming back to their ex with flowers, and the woman starts crying, and they live happily ever after. In actuality, this is not how it works because women do the choosing. You can't ask a woman for a relationship before she brings it to you, and you can't be the first one to try to reconcile the relationship after a breakup. When you do, you make women uncomfortable because their feelings aren't there yet. A man who wants a relationship more than a woman does is not a high-value male. High-value men want to date and stay single as long as they possibly can before the woman starts to ask, "Where is this going?" If you're a purple-pill guy interested in marriage someday, you shouldn't even consider asking the woman until she's throwing hints about marriage or flat-out asking, "What are we doing?" If you don't wait to hear that, the woman might agree to marry you out of obligation only to divorce you a couple years later because she never loved you to begin with. Women subconsciously progress the relationship at their own pace. If you're a guy who wants to progress the relationship, then try improving to become a high-value male to create feelings within the woman so that she wants to progress things. A man progressing things causes women to pull back or lose interest altogether.

43

Women Treat Every Man Differently

You say "needy"; I say "high interest." Once you become a high-value man with options, you better get used to women pursuing you heavily. This could come across as them being needy, but that would imply that she does this with every man she meets. That is the furthest thing from the truth. What I've learned from dealing with women in my life is that women act differently with different men. That same woman you're calling needy probably has ten other guys who've been trying to get a date with her for God knows how long. That same woman who gave it up to you the first night has twenty other guys who can't even get a callback. Men are so used to difficult women that they automatically assume a woman is easy if she sleeps with them soon after meeting. As you become a high-value man, you should start to demand this, as you're no longer going to wait three months to have sex with women. With that being said, there are some women who are needy, and there are some women who are slutty in the world, meaning they do act this way with every man they meet. Although there are these types of women in the world, as a high-value man, you should think it's you, and not her, first, but there is a way to tell if it's you or just her. Most women have been taught that men pursue, and even if she likes you a lot, she won't overpursue in the beginning. A woman who's double texting or calling right from the jump is definitely needy. It's virtually impossible to get a woman's interest that high initially, as women don't put as much emphasis on looks as men do. It usually takes a man's personality to raise a woman's interest high enough to where she's doing most of the pursuing. Women naturally try to screen out weak men by testing them to avoid sleeping with them. It's possible for a woman to test you over the course of a night out, and it is even possible if she came over to your place, because she could've tested you on the initial meeting or phone call. Only a complete slut would sleep with a man without testing his strength. If you were able to sleep with a woman without her testing you, then I guess it's safe to say she does that quite often. The only reason this should matter to you is if you're considering something long term with the woman. I personally see nothing wrong with a promiscuous woman, but we have a saying where I'm from: "Don't try to change a whore to a housewife." The reasoning for this is simple: when a woman shows a man that she's not a challenge, then he instantly knows he could never trust her fully. Whether you can change a whore to a housewife is debatable, but what can't be debated is that a man must be able to trust a woman, or the relationship is done, even if it's just the man's insecurity that causes the breakup.

44

What to Expect Once You Get into a Relationship

If you're a purple-pill guy, and you get into a relationship with a woman, it's commonplace to see a change in the woman's behavior in the same way a lot of men stop dating their woman or lose their masculine frame in a relationship. If you're a high-value male, and a woman perceives you as an alpha, then you can expect her to go all out to lure you into a relationship. This could include, but is not limited to, her cooking, being very feminine, and being very sexual in the bedroom. If a woman perceives you as a beta male, more than likely you had to convince her you were a good provider, and she did very little to win you over. In other words, women win over men they perceive as alpha males, but men who women perceive as beta males have to win women over. This is just another reason a man shouldn't get into a relationship with women who perceive him as a beta male. When a woman is actively seeking a beta-male provider, she might do some of the same things mentioned as she would for a man she perceives as an alpha in the short term to secure a relationship. If she has bigger aspirations, she might stay on her best behavior a little longer to secure marriage. The difference is when a woman is dating a man she perceives as an alpha male; as long as he maintains his swagger and masculine frame throughout the relationship, the woman never gets comfortable enough to stop doing what she initially did in the beginning because he knows how to keep her in a scarcity mind-set. When a woman is dating a man she perceives as a beta, he's typically the one in the scarcity mind-set due to the lack of affection a woman gives a man she perceives as a beta male. This lack of affection causes the man who the woman perceives as a beta male to always feel a sense of uncertainty. This allows the woman to control the relationship, and instead of her trying to keep him happy, he's trying to keep her happy. There's a couple of reasons women stop the special treatment once they get into a relationship with men they perceive as alpha males. For one, she knows she's your only source of sex if you're being monogamous. So this will be the equivalent of her trying to manipulate the relationship. This gives the woman tremendous leverage in the relationship. There's a myth that's floating around that says women love sex just as much as men. Anybody who knows anything about human sexuality knows this is a complete farce. Men have about eight times the amount of testosterone as women do. Testosterone is the main driver behind sexual desire. Women love sex, and that's a fact, but men would have sex 24/7 if they were given the chance. Relationships are about leverage, and whoever has the leverage controls the relationship. Unfortunately, women control most relationships due to this simple fact. Typical behavior you can expect is for her to not want sex as much as she once did as she "tries" to manipulate the relationship. If you're on your best behavior like a good boy, she'll give you a cookie. This good behavior is by letting her have her way. So if she has the power, how are you to get it back? The answer is simple: it's the same as what happens to your job if you stopped performing at work. You would get fired. Even if a woman isn't, let's say, being a bitch, a woman not doing what she did to get you is grounds for termination in my book. You can expect your woman to lose interest if you stop dating her, and a woman should expect you to want out if she's not doing what she previously did in the relationship. As a man, you have to let women know there's no lifetime achievement award; if she's not doing what she did previously in the relationship, you have to let her know that's not what you signed up for. Another reason you can expect women to not do what they did previously prior to the commitment is that giving a woman a relationship could be a sign to her that you're catching feelings. When you do anything that might be a sign that you're catching feelings, women naturally start to test boundaries. As a man, whenever you are tested by a woman in the slightest way, you have to always let her know anything less than complete compliance will not be tolerated.

CHAPTER

45

How Do I Decide Who Gets the Top Spot?

L ooks are very important to men and, upon initial approach, are usually the most important thing. When it comes to the women I'm currently dating, however, looks are no longer the determining factor, mainly because I don't date women below an eight in my eyes. I say "in my eyes" because looks are subjective. A dime to me might be a six to you. This is the same reason I theorize there is no universally alpha or beta male. When it comes to the women I'm dating, or what I like to call my rotation, compatibility is the most important thing in determining who gets the top spot. The top spot is usually Saturday night, as it's the night with the most couple activities and is schedule friendly, as most people work during the week. Personality is important, as it's always nice to hang out with a nice, feminine woman with high interest. The issue I have with trying to use personality as a determining factor as to who gets the top spot is if you don't have much in the way of compatibility, it can get pretty boring at times. When you're out with a woman who you are not compatible with but find highly attractive, and she has all the sweet, feminine qualities you want, sometimes it's hard to keep the conversation going. Maybe you're into sports, and she's into soap operas, but for whatever reason, due to a lack of compatibility, the relationship seems dull outside the bedroom. I'm not opposed to dating women I'm less compatible with, as I'm not looking for marriage, but when it comes to the top spot in my rotation, it has to be someone I can have an interesting conversation with. Looks are not even in the equation, as I would always rather spend more time with a woman I view as an eight and whom I am very compatible than spend time with a woman I view as a dime and am less compatible with. Don't confuse this with dating a woman I perceive as a five with compatibility. In that case, I would much rather date the dime and with less compatibility. You can't have sex 24/7; you have to talk to one another eventually. Looks, however, are always the most important thing when it comes to the quality of women I approach.

CHAPTER

46

It's All a Matter of Preferences

Some men are miffed at the notion that despite having their lives in order or having their stuff together, they still get rejected. Other men are miffed at the notion that despite being in great shape physically, they still get rejected. Well, besides the fact that looks are subjective, different women value different attributes in men. Some women are more turned on by a man with his life in order than they are by looks. These women could be looking for a beta-male provider or could just want a man who can bring what she brings to the table. A woman who makes $100,000 a year could just want a man who could meet her halfway. I can remember when I lived in a Brooklyn basement, and let me tell you, some women would run for the hills, while others didn't mind. The reason for that was the women who didn't mind their physical attraction for me overpowered their hypergamous nature. All women have different ideas about what's important to them, just like a man has different levels of what's important to him when it comes down to looks, personality, and responsibility. Some men will value a woman's looks, despite her being the biggest bitch this world has ever seen. I, however, value looks, but it won't matter how attractive you are if I don't like your personality or find you very irresponsible—like you purchase clothes when you're behind on your light bill. I can honestly say living in that basement cost me a lot of women, so I advise men to try to be the best version of themselves to give themselves the best chance to attract the most women they possible can. You're still going to get rejections, as everything in dating is subjective. What it means to have your life in order to one woman might not be the same for another woman. For instance, the woman at your gym might be impressed that you have a steady job, your own place, and reliable transportation. Nicole Murphy, however, who's been married to and dated multiple rich celebrities, might not be so impressed. What one woman might think is charming might be corny to another woman. The difference between being corny and charming can be something as simple as a woman's physical attraction level. When a woman has a high physical attraction level, everything you do and say within reason can be deemed to be charming. Looks aside, some women just have a different classification for what's charming. Some women prefer the smooth, laid-back, confident approach, while others prefer a more upbeat, jovial man. At the end of the day, it's all a numbers game, and the more of a social life you live, the better chance you have at attracting the quality of women you want. The reason I prefer to say you should live a social life as opposed to casually approaching women at random is the latter puts you in a position where your happiness depends on how many women you can attract, while the former suggests you just live a life of social abundance, and through the law of attraction, everything just happens naturally.

47

Women You Should Not Date

My niche in the dating community is mostly centered around raising a woman's interest level. I think it's also very important for men to have standards and not to simply date all women. It should always scare a man when a woman is pushing for a relationship from the start. I know a lot of men don't want to hear this, but women are the choosers. A woman should always have more options than a man does, unless the man is an A-list celebrity. Women are taught a man should prove his worth to them before they engage in sexual activity or a relationship with him. By proving yourself, I'm referring to passing her test, which tests your sexual market value. Men with options naturally pass the test due to having options, while men who don't have options fail women's tests. If the woman is looking for a provider, then she wants to see how good of a provider you are. She can determine this through the courting phase by how much money you spend on restaurants, trips, and so on. With women having so many options, it naturally makes them more selective. If a woman is pushing for a relationship from the start, it is a sign she doesn't have many options. Women who sleep with men without testing them are sluts. I call them this because they put no value on their bodies. I have no issue with a woman being as promiscuous as a man, but for God's sake, at least check to see if he has alpha characteristics. Women who want relationships without first weighing all of their options are women without options. Maybe a woman has sexual options, but not many men want anything else from her. This is a telltale sign of a woman with character flaws, because women with a lot of redeeming qualities usually have multiple men vying for their attention—and not just their sexual attention. Women without options are usually the women who bring nothing to the table but sex but are confused as to why men don't want anything from them but sex. If you're a guy and thinking to yourself, "Hey, I don't have anything to prove to women," that attitude is actually proving yourself to women because you don't think you have anything to prove to women. The guy who brags about his finances, cars, and vacations is the guy who actually fails because he's trying to prove himself to women. The guy who doesn't try to prove himself is the guy who actually is proving himself by having the mind-set of "Either I'm good enough, or I'm not." That shows an abundance mind-set, which shows options and a higher sexual market value. If a woman doesn't have options, then it must be for a reason, assuming she's on point physically. Women who are pushing for relationships from the start show they have a scarcity mind-set. A woman usually has multiple suitors unless they're morbidly obese, and even some of those women have options, as seen on *My 600-lb Life*. So if a woman doesn't have options, then you have to ask yourself why. I know you're probably thinking, "Hey, what if it's just high interest?" Good point, but I would counter that with the fact that initial high interest might make a woman want to jump in the sack with you, but getting into a monogamous relationship is something entirely different. Usually the reason a woman is pushing for a relationship from the get-go is that she has a bad reputation or is emotionally damaged. By "bad reputation," I'm referring to her promiscuous way of getting around. Nobody wants to wife the town whore. Typically, these women seek men who may not be familiar with their promiscuous ways. When I'm referencing being emotionally damaged, I'm referring to women who may have been hurt in the past or are lonely. A woman who's been hurt in the past may have trust issues or baggage. When a woman is trying to recover from a guy she might've developed an attachment to, but he doesn't want her, she'll try to find a rebound to keep her mind occupied. If you find yourself with a woman who's using you as a rebound, you always run the possibility of her hurting you if you get attached to her. I've had this happen several years ago when a woman got back with her ex. A woman will always retreat back to her ex when he wants her back if the attachment is still there. Your feelings won't matter. I think it's fair to say that most adults may have had their hearts broken at some point or another, but some carry this baggage longer than others. This baggage could lead to low self-esteem. A woman who still has trust and self-esteem issues will ultimately have a hard time trusting you, and vice versa. It's not your job to fix people. You'll never be able to give this type of woman enough validation to make her feel better about herself. You should strive to date women who are emotionally stable and happy and are not carrying emotional baggage.

You should not date women who constantly complain about a lack of communication. The reason I used the word "constantly" is that as a high-value man, you should expect to hear the occasional "Why do you never call me?" That's fine—and actually a good thing—as it shows the woman actually cares. It also shows you're providing the emotional turmoil women need to maintain their attraction to you. Hearing it every week or multiple times a week is something totally different. The issue with this is it starts to interfere with your purpose in life. Instead of focusing on your goals in life, you'll be focused on whether you called her enough that day. That's not even the bad part; the bad part is that no matter how much you communicate, it's never enough. This is why it's so important as a high-value man to date women on your same wavelength. Women who have goals and purpose in life are too preoccupied with their careers to worry about how much a man is calling them. I'm all for high-interest women, as they typically make things easy for the man, but some women cross the line and go straight into the needy category. A needy woman is almost as difficult to date as a woman with lower interest. At least the low-interest woman doesn't get on your nerves; she's just not interested.

Most women with children prefer not to introduce men to their children until they feel like the relationship is going somewhere. However, you may encounter women who try to introduce you to their children fairly quickly. You should never try to date these women. The reason for this is that they're trying to make you a stepdaddy within the first couple of weeks of dating. Some of these women even have the audacity to want to bring their children on the date. I feel like dating should be about getting to know the woman first, and if things go well, then maybe later you could meet her kids. Some women's rationale behind introducing a man quickly to their kids is that they don't want to invest much time into a man who doesn't click with their children. I would counter that argument with the fact that no man should want a woman who is actively looking for a relationship and vice versa. A person who is looking for a relationship is a person who isn't complete single and therefore is actively seeking someone to complete them. The type of people who look for love are typically the type of people who depend on you too much emotionally and time-wise. You should strive to date women who have a complete life made of friends, hobbies, and activities outside of you. These types of women tend to be better to date since they're already happy in their lives and not looking for someone to complete them. My advice, if you meet these types of women, is to maybe have fun for a little while, but I wouldn't ever consider putting them in my rotation.

Maya Angelou had a great phrase: "when people show you who they are, believe them." If you're a regular on the dating scene, you may run into some sarcastic women from time to time. A sarcastic woman may throw the occasional jabs your way via an insult or offensive statement. When you check her on it, she may give you the sarcastic laugh and the sarcastic woman's national anthem: "Why are you so serious? I'm just playing with you." Understand that if you decide to date this woman, her little insults and offensive statements will only get worse. After a while, you won't know when she's serious or just joking, but the thing is, she's always serious. A masculine frame doesn't stop these women, as they just have that smart, little mouth that always seems to have something sassy to say. A woman like this is technically gaslighting you, as you'll appear too sensitive when you check her on her sassy mouth. After a while, you may start to question yourself as to whether you are too sensitive. Dating individuals who try to make you question your emotional well-being is never a good idea.

Another type of woman every man should try to avoid is the materialistic woman. They're typically easy to spot because when you announce the date location, they usually have a rebuttal. I teach men to keep dates cheap, at least initially, to keep your investment down because there are no guarantees the two of you will even like each other. This won't work for materialistic women. Trust me when I say they'll conveniently always have a better spot in mind. From my experience, it does no good trying to go along with things in the hope of getting sex, as high-maintenance women typically make you work extremely hard to "earn" sex with them, and by "earn," I'm referring to spending money. A materialistic woman could find you attractive sexually, like your personality, and still not want to date you if you can't meet her requirements as far as providing. A woman who feels entitled to a fancy dinner on a first date is not the type of woman you want to date. It'll only be the beginning.

Dating Is for Betas

This might come as a surprise to a lot of my followers, but I actually enjoy going on dates with women. Whether you enjoy going on dates is all a matter of perception. If you perceive a date as only a means to get sex from women, then naturally you're going to hate the aspect of taking women on dates. This is the same reason a lot of men hate going to clubs. Instead of enjoying themselves, they see the club just as a means to meet women. If you think like I do, which is that the date is about me and not the woman, then you'll love taking women on dates. When I decide what I want to do Saturday evening after a long, hard week of grinding, I'm only concerned with what I want to do or where I want to eat. I'm only inviting a woman out as my company; if it's something she's not particularly fond of, then I don't all of a sudden change my plans for her. If you let the woman change your plans, then you're making the date about her. At this point, it shows the woman you're willing to do anything to spend time with her, which is a turnoff—unless she perceives you as a beta-male provider. If that's how she views you, then she expects you to change your plans. If I'm in that situation, I would either invite someone else or go alone. If any of you guys are wondering why I wouldn't just invite a guy friend out, if you've been following me for a while now, you would know that I'm not particularly fond of male companionship.

The reason I'm not fond of male companionship is quite simple: for all women's flaws, I would still rather hang with women over men any day of the week. I'm well aware that women can be hypergamous, emotional, and deceitful—and the list goes on—but I would much rather deal with women and their ways than men and their jealousy. If you have male friends, the biggest obstacle is avoiding jealousy. If both of you are losers or are fairly successful, there might not be much jealousy between you, but it is rare for two friends to be on the same wavelength. There's usually someone in the group doing better than the others, which in turn causes some kind of jealousy. A lot of individuals ignore jealous behavior from friends, but I simply can't do that. It doesn't even have to be monetary jealousy; it could be something as simple as one friend attracts more women than the other or sleeps with hotter chicks than the other. This has been my experience throughout my life when dealing with male companionship. If you're one of the lucky ones who actually has a supportive male cast, then consider yourself lucky and cherish those friendships, as I can speak from experience that they don't happen often. Some men have crappy friends but tolerate the jealousy because they rationalize that it's better than having no friends at all. These are the same guys, however, who also rationalize that it's better to keep an uncooperative female than to be alone. If you have a fear of being alone, then you're going to always have people in your life that disrespect you because you have no boundaries. Changing my plans to accommodate a woman would then mean the date is about her and not me. If I'm paying, then I'm going to go where I want to go. If the woman wants the date to be about her, then she should invite me out to where she wants to go.

There are a couple of other reasons a lot of men don't enjoy dates. First, they date women with very low interest, hoping to raise their interest over the course of the date; instead of trying to enjoy themselves on the date, they're fixated on their goal, which is to have sex. I advise men to talk on the phone with a woman first before going on a date to make sure she has adequate interest; a woman with less than average interest will sound very bored on the phone. In other words, the conversation will feel more like an interview than like a mutual conversation. If she sounds bored on the phone, then what makes you think she's going to all of a sudden be enthused on the date? When you're out with women who have genuine interest, dates are very fun to be on. A feminine woman makes the date easy, and it doesn't feel like you're on a job interview. Remember, a woman's feminine energy comes from her interest and attraction level. Another pitfall that men fall into is focusing too much on the end game instead of being present during the date. Being present means you're actually trying to get to know her and not just there to get sex. While I might be against monogamous relationships, I actually like women. The reason a lot of men don't like women is that they spend too much time chasing women with low interest or women who are attention whores. Women who actually like you, which creates feminine energy, are very fun to be around. Another reason some men hate women is they hate the aspect of women having the power to choose. A lot of men hate the fact that women will always have more options than men do. Even if the woman makes minimum wage and is slightly overweight, she'll have more options than a multimillionaire with a six-pack. The reason women will always have more options than men do has more to do with men than it does with women. Men by and large will sleep with anything that moves as long as she looks halfway decent. Women, however, typically have some standards. Even the town slut will only sleep with men she finds very desirable. Men have very low standards as to whom they would sleep with, and this gives the women more options. A lot of men hate to come to grips with this aspect of sexual relations between men and women.

This inability to deal with reality often causes some men to hate women. These low standards are often why the average woman will always have more of an abundance mind-set than the average man does. In addition, I'm not against going out to eat alone. My rationalization is, why would I go out alone when I have women whom I'm interested in I could take out? If I don't have a particular woman I'm interested in, then by no means am I afraid to go to dinner by myself.

49

You're Going to Die Old and Lonely

If you're a heterosexual man who chooses to live a bachelor's lifestyle, then I'm sure you've heard the phrase "You're going to die old and lonely" at least once in your life. As a man, you can expect to be shamed when you don't conform to society's social programming. Anytime you think for yourself as opposed to living like a sheep and following the herd, you should expect to be shamed. Women are master manipulators, and when something doesn't benefit them, they resort to shaming tactics. The funny thing is, men who've bought into this way of thinking will also shame you. In fact, you should expect more shaming tactics from men than from women if you're a red-pill man. I think this comes from jealousy within those men. When a man is single and free to do as he pleases, I think men who are in relationships deep down envy this type of man. They wish they could live a life of freedom without feeling lonely, and by freedom, I'm referring to the ability to make all your choices on your own. Any man who's in a relationship can attest to the fact that although he may be an adult, once you're in a committed relationship, especially if you're married or living together, you no longer make decisions on your own. You have to weigh your woman's opinion too. So if you're a man who's thinking about quitting your job to pursue your passion in life, you can't do that without talking it over with your girlfriend or wife. You can try to make decisions of this nature on your own, but it can lead to a lot of cold nights, if you get what I'm saying. When you're single and not into monogamous relationships, you can make life-altering decisions void of anyone's opinions. This is why I think men who *need* relationships develop jealousy toward men who don't. That was not a mistake when I used the word "need." Some men *need* a relationship because they can't stand the thought of being alone. As a man who doesn't conform to society's standards, you may hear this from beta males. The reason I refer to them as beta males is that alpha males don't capitulate to the masses. Alpha males do their own thing and don't let others influence them. Living a bachelor's lifestyle doesn't automatically make you an alpha male, because there are a lot of married alpha males; being your own man does. You can be married or in a monogamous relationship and still be considered an alpha male, but it has to be something that you wanted to do and not something a woman gave you an ultimatum to do or because you wanted to keep her from seeing other men. This is why I commonly refer to men who cheat in monogamous relationships as the "world's biggest cockblockers." Men who cheat in monogamous relationships are the world's biggest simps. I say this because they didn't get into a monogamous relationship because it's something they wanted to do but rather to simply prevent the woman from sleeping with other men. There are a couple of reasons that women and beta males shame men who choose to live a bachelor lifestyle. The women do it because it doesn't benefit them. The female narrative is to have fun with men they perceive as alpha males in their prime years only to settle down with men they perceive as beta males once the women have matured and are ready to start a family, assuming they are unable to find an all-around alpha male to settle down with. Maybe a woman has a kid or two by a man she perceived as an alpha and now wants a man she perceives as a beta male to pick up the tab. Men either wander in their early years trying to get laid as much as possible or build their careers. Some men can actually accomplish these tasks simultaneously, but usually you have to pick one or the other. Men who spent their early years chasing women are usually the ones who later in life apply to the saying "You're going to die old and lonely." Let me explain. If you spend your early years pursuing women instead of focusing on building yourself up, you're not going to have much value once you reach forty years of age. By that point, you're usually not attractive enough to attract the younger women as you once were, and the women your age are more about stability by that point. So in that case, yes, you very well may die old and lonely because your sexual market value is very low since you're not as attractive as you once were and don't have the finances that women who are ready to settle down are looking for. These men still have their charisma and swagger, but I think it's fair to say that an older man with limited finances might not have the same confidence level that he once did. That's only human nature, as I don't think it's possible for a forty-year-old woman to have the same confidence she once did. Let's be honest for a second; a lot of your confidence comes from external validation. People can try to deny this, but it's the truth. If you turn a lot of heads when you walk down the street, then I think it's fair to say your confidence is going to be a little higher than someone who doesn't. Of course, it's always better if your confidence comes from internal sources rather than external ones, but this just isn't always the case. I know there are always going to be outliers, and there are some guys who are able to maintain their sex appeal well into their forties and beyond. But you shouldn't count on this being the norm. Additionally, some older women might not care if you're not exactly swimming in money in your forties, but the number of women who consider you to be a viable option greatly decreases in that situation, so you do run the risk of dying old and lonely. I must also bring up the fact that you could get married to a woman and then get a divorce, leaving you destitute anyway. However, if you spent your early years chasing success, you shouldn't have this issue as long as you developed the right mind-set along the way. A man with his life in order in his later years not only makes himself viable to younger women, as seen with Hugh Hefner, but also makes himself viable to older women looking for stability. I'm not opposed to dating women who view you as a beta-male provider; I'm just opposed to getting into a monogamous relationship with women who view you as a beta-male provider. Quite frankly, I wouldn't even put a woman who views me as a beta-male provider in my rotation. A man who has his life in order should naturally be confident based on the number of options he has, but some men lack this confidence due to a lack of socializing that typically happens in a person's later years. As we age, we usually become homebodies. If you're a man who has his life in order and can manage to maintain an active social life, you shouldn't have an issue maintaining the confidence needed to give you the swagger to attract women even in your elderly state. Remember, success, coupled with an active social life, prevents scarcity.

50

Location, Location, Location

Something that is often overlooked is your location. You can be following your purpose all you want, but if you live in a slow city or town with what seems like five women in it, it's very easy to fall into a scarcity mind-set. This lack of activity can make you feel like you're compelled to stay in a toxic relationship or overpursue a woman you're dating. Whenever a man isn't living with the mind-set of abundance, bad things start happening. The abundance mind-set will not only improve your social life but also improve your career, as more often than not, a more vibrant city has more career opportunities. You have to live in a place that actually has places to socialize. I'm from a small town myself, so I know firsthand the challenges facing a man in this situation. If you live in a small, boring town with limited options, my advice to you would be to start planning your escape. Maybe this takes a year or two to accomplish, but I would start working on this immediately. Living in a small town with nothing to do can make you feel lonely. There's only so much time you can give to your purpose before you need a mental break. How are you supposed to live an active social life if there's nothing to do? A lot of men are going to read this and think to themselves, "My career is here," but I would counter that statement by saying that's not the only job you can get. What I learned about human beings in my nearly forty years on this earth is that most people would rather complain about something than come up with solutions. Another thing I've learned is that nothing fixes itself; you have to fix the situation. So either you can stay where your job is and be isolated or you can move, find another job, and live a social life of abundance. I can't speak for everybody, but I was miserable at times living in a small town with limited things to do. Of course, you could just travel to the nearest big town, but I would then ask, why not just move there instead? Whatever you're saving on rent by living farther away from the city would surely be negated by driving back and forth anyway. As a high-value man, time is your biggest asset, not money. High-value men buy time, while low-value men sell time. What I mean by this is that people with a high-value mind-set have figured out that it's better to pay a little more for rent and spend more time working than to spend that time they otherwise would commuting two hours a day because they live farther away from the city. If instead of spending two hours a day five days a week commuting, you spent that time working, you've more than made up for the extra price in rent. Your location also matters in that it gets women comfortable. You can have as much game and confidence as you want, but if you can't make a woman feel comfortable, then nothing will happen sexually. I'm not saying you have to live at the Ritz-Carlton to make a woman feel comfortable, but you can't live in a doghouse either. I'm not talking about how nice your crib is, although that helps, I'm referring to a woman needing privacy and the assurance of safety. As with most things regarding dating, some women won't mind if you live in a house full of relatives or roommates, while some will. I will say this, though: you undoubtedly will be leaving a lot of women on the table if you don't live alone. Some women feel insecure about everyday human activities, such as using the restroom or having sex, while friends and relatives are in the next room. Some women simply can't get in the mood with other individuals, particularly adults, in the next room. What if they hear her for God's sake? My advice to men has always been and will continue to be to focus on improving your living situation first; therefore, when you do attract women, it will be easier to seal the deal. In my opinion, the last thing a man who doesn't have his own place should be focusing on is dating. If this is you, then your priorities are all out of whack.

51

How to Get a Woman to Chase You

A lot of men are fascinated with the thought of a woman chasing them. If a woman is chasing you, it does give you this feeling of superiority and attractiveness. It's also a great indicator of interest in most cases; after all, you could just be dealing with a lunatic who gets too attached to every man she dates. While being chased is the ideal situation for any man, the facts of the matter are that the only way to get a woman to chase you really has nothing to do with you. It's really more about her. First off, it's impossible to get a strong-minded woman to chase you. A woman who values herself and has the mind-set of abundance would never chase a man, no matter how much he tries to manipulate the situation. You can pull back and work on your purpose twenty-four hours a day, and she still won't chase. That's because people who value themselves and live in a mind-set of abundance would never chase someone. This is why I teach high-value principles. Women will try to manipulate you with all the little games they play, but when you respect yourself as a man, you simply won't chase. This is why I don't teach manipulation but rather the mind-set that you need to succeed in dating. The mind-set you need is a mind-set of abundance. Even if the woman had crazy-high interest, she wouldn't chase you because her pride overrides her interest level. A lot of men don't have this pride, however, and start chasing once a woman pulls back. I can tell you firsthand I've had women I had a very high attraction and interest in that tried to manipulate me, but I'm too mentally strong for manipulation. Manipulation only works on weak individuals. The other aspect is that no matter what you do, there are some women whose attraction level you will never be able to get high enough in order for them to chase you, even if they are mentally weak. Sometimes you aren't going to be able to raise every woman's interest level to the extreme, even if you're doing and saying all the right things. In this situation, it's more about compatibility than being a high-value man. You could literally do everything right and never get a woman's interest to extreme levels. Then she meets another guy after you who doesn't have half of what you have, and she's all over him. That's because he's more compatible with her in what drives her emotions crazy. This is where living a social life of abundance comes in handy: you meet enough women to where you actually meet a woman you just do it for without having to try that hard. You can try to be as charming as you want to be, but the woman might not find you that charming. Remember, everything in dating is subjective. Have you ever wondered why some women are pursuing you right from the jump, while others aren't? That's called "catching lightning in a bottle," and you just do it for her. Sometimes you just get lucky and meet a woman who you just do it for without really trying that much.

52

Things a Man Should Never Do with a Woman

W omen are irrational, while men are supposed to be rational. Women are emotional, while men are supposed to be reserved. Women gossip, while men supposedly don't. I used the phrase "supposed to" because, unfortunately, a lot of men have more estrogen than women do. As a man, you shouldn't be a Chatty Patty, or a man who gossips. You can't expect women to do explicit things with you in the bedroom if you're the type of guy who tells everyone everybody's business—including your own. It's also a sign of feminine energy, which enhances the chances of your woman moving into her masculine energy. As a man, it's always good practice to say as little as possible. You want to be a mystery and have your woman wondering what you're thinking. Trust is hard to develop but not hard to lose; one slip of the tongue to the wrong person could prevent your woman from trusting you again. I had a woman once who would tell all our business to her family members. It got to a point where I didn't tell her anything that I had going on personally. The trust had been broken, and when the trust is gone, the relationship, monogamous or not, is soon to follow.

Never try to sell yourself to a woman, and by "sell yourself," I'm referring to selling her on your sexual market value. Technically, a date is a way for a man to sell himself to a woman, but the best way to sell yourself is by not trying to sell yourself. Once you start trying to sell yourself, you're subconsciously informing the woman that she has a higher value than you do, and therefore you have to tell her all the great things you have going on. Let women discover your successes on their own. One way men try to sell themselves to a woman is by trying to inform the woman of their financial status. This is taking the beta-male provider route. Men must understand that women don't respect "tricks." Tricks are men who spend all their money to get female companionship, either covertly or overtly. The reason women don't respect this kind of man is that he doesn't respect himself. That's the same reason a woman can't respect a man who doesn't have the strength to walk away when she's disrespecting him. You can't expect anyone to respect you, man or woman, if you don't respect yourself. In my opinion, there's nothing wrong with "peacocking." Peacocking is when a man dresses nice or has a nice ride. A lot of men might try to proclaim themselves peacocking as things they bought for themselves but subconsciously men buy nice things to attract the highest-quality female they can just like women subconsciously wear sexy clothing to attract the highest-quality mate they can. Even if you're in a happy monogamous relationship or marriage, your instincts to attract the highest-quality mate never ceases. You should let your success speak for itself; you don't have to broadcast it. Women are very observant of those types of things. Another way men try to sell themselves is by namedropping or bragging about past relationships with other beautiful women. Men do this to try to show they're used to her caliber of women. This is definitely a turnoff, as women don't like to sleep with men who brag about the notches they have in their belts, as women intuitively know these men will do the same if they sleep with these men. A woman can tell if you're successful with other women just by you passing her test. There's no need to tell a woman about past women you've dated. It actually can have an adverse effect, as women perceive men who try to brag as insecure men hiding behind their success.

53

Alpha Male Strategies' Male Hierarchy

break down men into six categories. Before I tell you the six classifications for my male archetypes, I want to make something abundantly clear. Each category a man could be in is mainly based on his mind-set and how he sees himself. The difference between a man who gets women to give him money and a man who feels no woman on earth wants him is the difference in how they view themselves and not how women view them. The two primary categories are alpha and beta males. The six categories are subcategories of these two, since all these archetypes fall under one of the two main categories.

My first archetype category is the pimp. This is the guy who's able to manipulate women into giving him money. This is not about him being lazy but rather about the entitlement he feels. The idea of the sexual marketplace is a man is supposed to provide protection and stability for a woman in order for her to consider him to be a candidate sexually. A lot of individuals would probably say this has more to do with social programming, but I beg to differ. Women are the weaker sex, so it stands to reason that back in the prehistoric days, women looked to men to provide these two essential things for survival. The pimp, however, puts more value on himself as a man and thinks he should be compensated for his attention. A pimp has the mind-set that a woman's sexual availability isn't worth his attention by itself. I know the word "pimp" is synonymous with getting women to sell their bodies in order to provide the man with money, but in the business world, it doesn't matter how the woman gets the money. Usually women have regular nine-to-five jobs to provide financially for the man. Do not confuse the pimp with a kept man. In this situation, he's basically traded gender roles with the woman in a relationship. The kept man usually does the house chores, runs errands, and clean to earn his keep. With the pimp, just his presence is enough. A lot of men look down on a man like this and view him as a lazy bum, but this is basically because men have been programmed to provide for women, so while I do believe there was a time when men were needed to provide, this doesn't hold true today. Women are no longer dependent on a man for resources and protection, as a lot of women make their own money. Women making their own money is probably the biggest reason you see so many sexually frustrated men today. When women were totally dependent on men, even the lamest men were guaranteed to have sex so long as he had something to offer monetarily. Women making their own money these days has allowed a lot of women to sleep with men depending on their sexual desires rather than out of necessity and survival. Before the sexual revolution started, any man would have had just as good a chance as any smooth-talking heartthrob. The sexual revolution and feminism have severely hurt men who perceive themselves as beta males because women were no longer required to wait until marriage to have sex. This allowed women to sleep with men who perceived themselves as alpha males with impunity. Additionally, these men were hurt because feminism made it OK for women to have jobs and provide for themselves. This freedom devalued the importance of being a beta-male provider.

Being a dating coach for a couple of years now, I've noticed that everybody thinks they're an alpha male. To be honest, the only true alpha males are famous, rich male celebrities with an abundance mind-set. The reason I added "abundance mind-set" to the description of a true alpha male is that there are male celebrities who still live in scarcity despite having women throw themselves at them. The term "alpha male" has been distorted and watered down over the years. True alpha males have women chasing them. True alpha males are the type of men who women have threesomes with regularly and sleep with solely based on their status. The term "alpha male" originally was used to categorize men who led the pack and slept with all the women. Women pursued them in the hope of having their offspring to replicate their genetics. By this definition, even I'm not a true alpha male. I have women who send me choosing signals, but true alpha males have women throwing themselves at them. All famous, rich celebrities aren't alpha males, as some men still have the beta-male mind-set despite obtaining riches and fame. The beta mind-set is when, despite having fame and riches, they still think women have more value than they do, causing them to act like betas. The only problem a true alpha male has with women is which woman he wants to sleep with that day. True alpha males are alpha males due more to their status than to their resources. Status will always be the number one characteristic a man could have with women, as it's the highest form of social proof. "Alpha male" also refers to the context and frame you're dealing with. For instance, the captain of the football team might be the alpha male on campus, but outside that campus, he's a regular Joe because he no longer has that status at his disposal. A manager at a job might be the alpha male to employees, specifically the female employees, but once he clocks out, he's a regular Joe. I think we've all seen how women clamor to sleep with or date the boss so as long as he had an alpha mind-set.

I call these types of alpha males "situational alpha males." I label them this because true alpha males have women pursuing them in any situation. A lot of men who were the man in college found it a lot harder to attract women once they graduated. Now that I've gotten what a true alpha male is out the way, I will tell you what an alpha male is for the other 99 percent of men on earth, including myself. I classify these men as "all-around alpha males." These men are self-employed and are able to sleep with women without providing anything financially. Maybe you meet them for a drink, but by and large, you don't do anything extraordinary to sleep with women. For the guys who might claim themselves to be alpha males while working for someone else, I would counter that by suggesting that no true alpha male would work for someone else long term. If you're working for someone else with the goal of starting your own business, then that's fine, but if you're content with being an employee, there's no way you can classify yourself as an all-around alpha male. One of the biggest characteristics of being an all-around alpha male is risk taking. If you're content with being an employee, then that in itself shows you're not a risk taker. Men who perceive themselves as alpha males just have a hard time taking orders from someone else.

The next category is probably better suited for men who either struggle financially or work for someone else but have no trouble sleeping with women without providing anything financially. I refer to them as the "sexual alpha males." These are the men that can sweet talk the pants off of most of the women they meet. This sweet-talking ability comes from a confidence in themselves that most men couldn't imagine. The difference between the sexual alpha and the pimp is the pimp gets money from women, while the sexual alpha just gets sex. It takes a little more game to get a woman to give you money than to just get sex. It also takes a different mind-set, as the pimp believes his time is worth more than just sex. It takes a lot of confidence in one's ability to achieve that perfect pitch in one's voice to turn women on. It's not an outright skill, but rather a trait any man could have once he truly develops confidence in himself. Understand that if you take women out on fancy dates to impress them in order to sleep with them, then you are providing something. I do take women on nice dates, but it's after we've slept together, and it's something I want to do, and she's just my company. It really just boils down to mind-set and motive. Either you go on nice dates because it's something you truly want to do, which means it's about you, or you can do it because you're trying to impress the woman. The downside to this category other than the obvious (of these men not having their lives in order) is that a woman's attraction is 100 percent dependent on their swagger, since they have nothing to provide. That means that if they ever catch feelings or lose their confidence, they won't have anything else to maintain the woman's attraction. This mind-set also limits the number of women who see them as viable. A lot of women won't give you the time of day if you don't have your life in order, no matter how charismatic they may find you.

A "sexual beta" is the type of man who kicks butt in the business world but suffers in the romance department. A sexual beta might be the CEO of a Fortune 500 company but hasn't had any women interested in him romantically for months at a time. Even when he does get women to be interested in him, it's based solely on his resources and has very little to do with him. This lack of sexual interest causes him to rely more and more on his resources, which then causes him to never develop the swagger needed to be successful with women. From my experience, most sexual betas seem to be content with this arraignment, as their social programming for being a provider overrules any rational thought otherwise. This just goes to show you that despite having status and financial success, nothing overrides a man's perception of himself and his mind-set. I've seen men with fame and riches act like they were just happy to have some woman with a cute face who makes minimum wage give them the time of day. It's quite amazing to see how a man in one aspect of his life could be so risk taking and optimistic but so cowardly and pessimistic in another. My theory for this is some men just don't want to accept that beauty is in the eyes of the beholder. Most men have this perception of what is considered good looking, and since they don't meet those criteria, they automatically assume they're destined to be a beta-male provider. While I do agree that there are some standards of beauty that are "widely" accepted, the key thing to note is that you're always beautiful to someone somewhere, no matter how you look. The upside to being a beta-male provider is that depending on what you make financially, you could possibly sleep with the same caliber of women as the men who perceive themselves alpha males do. Admittedly, it would be for different reasons, and it wouldn't feel the same, but the facts remain the same. There are a lot of men who perceive themselves as beta males who sleep with very beautiful women simply because they are successful.

Some men have no confidence in themselves entirely. I classify these men as "all-around beta males." An all-around beta male is an individual who either struggles financially or just accepts his fate as being an employee for the rest of his life while he also struggles in the romance department. The reason these guys struggle with women is directly linked to their financial situation. When a man perceives himself as a beta male and is not successful, it's only natural for him to struggle with women, since his confidence level is directly linked to what he can provide financially. As I've mentioned before, I firmly believe that any man can go from any category he wants; it's really just a matter of mind-set. However, these are the men who let an insecurity they have make them feel like betas. It's like how some people who are born poor think they have to stay poor. You can go from poor to rich if you're willing to put the work in, and you can go from a beta mind-set to an alpha mind-set if you change your outlook on life. I think I'm alpha; therefore, I am alpha. I don't really care how anyone else views me. You think you're beta; therefore, you're beta. It's all a matter of perception. Every woman I date doesn't view me as an alpha male; therefore, I don't date them very long, as I want to spend the majority of my time dating women who view me as an alpha male. These men usually end up with women they really aren't that attracted to but figure something is better than nothing. Have you ever wondered why your best friend is married to a woman twice his body weight? I can guarantee you that he didn't have many women who looked like Halle Berry in his phone book. I know a lot of men who perceive themselves as beta males who have some charisma, but their scarcity mind-set overrides it.

My last archetype is the "incel," which stands for "involuntary celibate." Incels can be well off financially, but due to their lack of social skills and awareness, they're unable to attract a woman, or many friends for that matter. This means the man wants to engage in sexual activity but is unable to find women to sleep with him. My suggestion to this type of individual would be to improve themselves, but a lot of incels aren't even what the average person would consider bad-looking or destitute guys. From my observation, most incels lack the social skills needed to attract women. Based on the videos I've seen online from incels, the men obviously have a lack of social skills and awareness. As a man, if you lack social skills and awareness, you're going to come across as creepy to women. By "creepy," I'm referring to awkwardness when you're in the vicinity of women. This is usually due to a lack of socializing, causing you to overly stare or come across as weird when you're in the proximity of women. A lot of the time, whether you're coming across as creepy is based on the woman's attraction level toward you, but that's not always the case. When a man lacks an adequate social life, he lacks the social skills needed to not stare too hard, which sends off the signals of a creep. This is creepy to women because you stare but don't make a move. This creeps women out because you seem interested, but you never say anything. This is the same situation you see when people lack proper social lives, and when they come in contact with others, they act overly excited, causing them to talk too much. This overtalking can prevent you from making friends, causing the cycle to constantly repeat itself, since you don't have many, if any, friends. What's my suggestion? Put the video games down, get out of the house, and live a social life. The problem isn't going to fix itself; you have to fix it. You have to socialize to develop social skills and awareness.

Only Red- and Purple-Pill Men Can Be Alpha Males

A major component to having so many women perceive you as a beta male is your ignorance toward the female nature. Red-pill men generally have a good understanding of female nature and thus don't make silly mistakes, like overpursuing. Red-pill men know women are dating multiple men when they meet them; therefore, they aren't surprised when a woman just up and disappears out of their life. Being red pill isn't the only factor in becoming a man who perceives himself as an alpha male, but it is, however, a major component. Most men who perceive themselves as alpha males actually got their red-pill knowledge from sleeping with women in relationships rather than from heartbreak. I'm aware that some of you may have become red pill after going through heartbreak, but a lot of men like myself got it from either watching how females in our families treated the men they would date or sleeping with women in relationships. The reason being red pill is such a major component to becoming a man who perceives himself as an alpha male is that once you understand female nature, you're incapable of falling into a scarcity mind-set because you now know how female minds operate. This newfound knowledge prevents you from ever giving yourself 100 percent to a female, therefore preventing you from falling into a scarcity mind-set. Don't think being red pill means you're an alpha male. You can be a red-pill beta male. What I am saying, however, is that you can't be an alpha male without being red pill. Men who perceive themselves as betas can still be red pill and beta because they still may have insecurities about themselves that prevent them from developing an abundance mind-set despite their knowledge about the female nature. Insecurities a man has in himself are and always will be the greatest determinant of how a man views himself. Combine this with a lack of a social life, and you have the recipe for a man living with a scarcity mind-set. For instance, I don't let my receding hairline or speech impediment cause me to lose confidence in myself or make me feel less attractive to women. Men who perceive themselves as beta males but are red-pill aware let insecurities like height and a larger nose kill their self-esteem. This, in turn, puts them in a scarcity mind-set. A red-pill alpha male never falls into scarcity because even when he meets a woman that seems perfect, he understands that the woman is not his but rather that it's just his turn. A scarcity mind-set is the biggest factor in why some men perceive themselves as beta males. Red-pill men don't believe in "the one" myth because they understand women can't fight against their hypergamous nature.

CHAPTER

55

Confidence Is Not Universal

Dating coaches always emphasize the importance of confidence, as if confidence is some magical substance you can buy at the store. What is confidence, and where does it come from? Why are some men confident, while others aren't? Well, I don't believe there's such a thing as a universally confident man. I believe confidence is a situational thing, and it wanes from time to time. Success, familiarity, and a mind-set of abundance cause us to have confidence in different situations. There's no doubt that if you have a lot of success with women, you're going to be confident with women, but what if the last twenty women you approached rejected you? How are you to remain confident? This is where the mind-set of abundance comes into play. You can take a player like Kobe Bryant, who was a volume shooter; he would never let a couple bad shots, or bad games for that matter, lower his confidence—or did it? I would make the assertion that a couple of bad games would lower any man's confidence temporarily. The difference is that Kobe knows what a lot of men who have success with women, or success with anything for that matter, know: it's just a matter of time before he's making shots again. The law of averages says that you're bound to have a bad game here and there, or in the example of approaching and dating women, you're bound to run into a cold streak eventually, no matter who you are. Everybody's confidence goes up and down from time to time just depending on how much success they're having at any given point in time in a particular activity, but some seem to understand the law of averages, while others don't. I really can't give you a good explanation as to why some people aren't able to develop this mind-set of abundance, while others, with just a little self-improvement, are. The only thing I can come up with is that some men have been so socially programmed to what truly attracts women that they just give up. I won't kid you and act like there isn't a general guideline to what's a good-looking man because that would be disingenuous, but the facts remain the same: you don't need two billion women to find you attractive. All you need is a few women to find you attractive. I won't say one woman because the odds of you finding that one woman would be virtually impossible. The reason I say that confidence is not universal is that the same guy who lacks confidence with women might be confident in almost every other aspect of his life. I've had male friends who were very confident in approaching women but who lacked that same confidence in virtually every other aspect of life. That assertion leads me to believe that confidence isn't really about confidence at all but rather not having a fear of failure or rejection. A lot of men have this fear of being rejected when approaching women. That's because they take the rejection as a judgment as to who they are as an individual, when in fact timing is and always will be the biggest factor when determining whether you get rejected by women. Had you met that same woman a month earlier or a month later, she might've been open to dating you, but maybe right now, she's not in the right frame of mind to date, or maybe she just had a long day at work, and you approached her on the wrong day despite you being her type physically. For the men who are confused as to why confidence is so attractive to women, the answer is pretty simple. When a man has confidence, women instinctively know that confidence must come from somewhere. Women know a man who has confidence must be successful with women, hence the confidence he exudes. A man's confidence level is directly linked to his sexual market value. A man who's confident must have options. As I've said before, a man's sexual market value is based on the highest-quality female he can attract. Muscles and money have nothing to do with a man's sexual market value directly. They can indirectly have an effect on his sexual market value by increasing his confidence, which in turn attracts a highly attractive female, but that's about it. If money and muscles were responsible for a man's sexual market value, then why are there men with money and muscles who struggle with women? The reason men with money and muscles struggle with women is that despite the appearance of being a confident man, insecurities still linger inside. Money can't hide your insecurities. In fact, money makes your insecurities more prominent because you'll have a tendency to lead with your wallet instead of with your personality. The only thing that can cause a man to lose his insecurities is to learn how to accept his flaws as a human being. We all have flaws; even that drop-dead gorgeous woman at your gym has flaws. If you don't think women have insecurities, then think again. Pretty much every woman on reality TV has had some kind of cosmetic surgery done. When a man lacks confidence, he's subconsciously sending a message to the woman that he's not very successful with women, hence the lack of confidence. You should never hesitate when you want to approach a woman. Hesitation is a sign of a man who doubts himself. The woman intuitively knows you must get rejected quite often or are not very successful with women to doubt yourself, which is a turnoff. Trust me when I say a woman knows when you want to approach her. That twenty minutes it took you to build up your courage to approach could cost you a great opportunity with a woman. When a woman meets you initially, more often than not she's unaware of your sexual market value. The only thing women can use to gauge it is your confidence level. They gauge your confidence level by your tone, body language, eye contact, and conversational skill.

Women Also Play the Game

Contrary to popular belief, you can have too much of an abundance mind-set. As with everything in life, too much of anything is not good. One thing that is all too common is for men to go from one extreme to the other. Men go from blowing up a woman's phone to waiting two weeks to ask her out again. Either scenario is ideal, but when done with the correct balance, you will get your desired outcome. I teach men to have an abundance mind-set, which keeps you from pursuing women with below-average or lukewarm interest. Lukewarm interest is when a woman sees you as a five or six on a scale of one to ten. If you're a beginner, then it might be in your best interest to try to raise a woman's lukewarm interest, but once you recognize yourself as a high-value man, you simply won't have time to raise women's lukewarm interest. This is why I refer to this book as "advanced game." My initial book was more about the basics. Beginner or advanced, no man should deal with women who have an interest level below a five. What I've come to see is that men have taken my teachings and gone overboard as to what's acceptable interest. Men shouldn't expect women to act overly excited initially even if they are highly interested. Some women even go to the extreme of canceling dates because they've been taught to play hard to get. Those kinds of women are doing the same thing men who wait two weeks to ask a woman out again are doing, and that's going to the extreme when it's not necessary. When a woman cancels a date on me, that's not a signal to me to try harder, and when you wait two weeks to ask a woman out again, that's too extreme. If one of those women meets one of the men who follows my teachings, she'll quickly find out that man is not about to pursue her. Men have to understand that women play the game too. Women are well aware of the difference between how a man treats them when he's unsure of their interest level and when he makes it blatantly obvious. Men tend to take a woman who shows her interest for granted, thus preventing her from being courted properly as she desires. I can attest to the fact that I've treated women when I was unsure of their interest level better than I treated the women who made their interest obvious. If a woman isn't pursuing you, that shouldn't be grounds to stop pursuing her, unless you have a woman who you're more interested in or you are just no longer interested in her. The woman could have legitimate interest but is simply concealing her interest in the hope of creating value. You'll know when women don't have or have lost interest because they'll stop making themselves available. I want men to develop an abundance mind-set, but if you're moving on from women who aren't doing backflips on dates, then you could very well be missing out on some favorable dating situations. You should also have the confidence that you have the ability to raise any woman's interest so long as it's not too low to begin with. The reason for this is that the lower her initial attraction, the more you have to invest initially. This means it will take more dates and more of your nonsexual attention to raise her interest to where she's comfortable sleeping with you. The abundance mind-set comes into play when you're dealing with women who flake on dates, won't set dates, try to reschedule dates constantly, or try to use you as a backup plan. You'll recognize this by the famous low-interest phrases women use: "We'll see," or "I'll let you know." My motto is as long as she's making dates, and the dates are progressing, then keep pursuing. Just make sure she's initiating contact from time to time too. As I've already stated, when a woman wants you, she'll initiate contact no matter how structured she is. That dates progress should be emphasized because you have women out there who will let you take them out repeatedly even though they have no romantic interest in you. I can't tell you how many possible great experiences I've blown due to having such high standards from women on the initial meetings when the women were probably just playing the game.

57

Losing Sexual Market Value over Time

A common fear of men is the phrase "You're going to die old and lonely." The good news for men is that women don't put nearly as much emphasis on looks as we do. Before you get overly excited, you must understand that just because women don't put as much emphasis on looks as we do, looks do matter to women, especially initially because you have to meet their minimum attraction level. Thinking anything different would be delusional. A man's sex appeal is the most important attribute, outside of status, to women. As only a select few men have the status of a celebrity, sex appeal is going to be the biggest attraction to women for 99 percent of men. Sex appeal is a combination of a lot of factors, such as confidence, charisma, swagger, and looks. I don't consider swagger and confidence the same because I classify swagger as the way a man carries himself—particularly the way he walks. Confidence is just your state of being. Some men just have more of a swagger when they carry themselves. It's virtually impossible for a man's appearance to improve with age unless he wasn't optimizing his appearance when he was younger, such as by carrying excess weight, having poor fashion sense, and so on. As with anything, there, of course, will always be outliers who were able to maintain, if not improve, their appearance with aging.

The best way to keep your sexual market value as high as possible while aging is to maintain a healthy weight. Unwanted fat adds a lot of years to your appearance besides the fact that it's just not attractive to a majority of women. Fat used to be associated with wealth centuries ago, but today it's mostly associated with laziness and low self-esteem. The average woman is attracted to the opposite of her. Women's bodies are soft, and men's bodies are supposed to be hard. As with any measure of attractiveness, while the overwhelming majority of the public might find one particular trait attractive, there will always be outliers. There are women out there who like fat men. Some of these women might prefer fat men because they feel fat men have far fewer options than fit men, thus emphasizing the insecurities they may have, but let's also keep in mind that there are different strokes for different folks. Some women are genuinely attracted to fat men. Feminine women are attracted to masculine men, and soft women largely aren't attracted to men softer than they are. You should strive to eat a well-balanced diet of green vegetables, lean proteins, and healthy fats and drink plenty of water. Green vegetables provide antioxidants that slow down the aging process. Water keeps your skin hydrated, which slows the aging process. The more acidic things you put into your body, the faster you're going to age your skin. Keep in mind that all this just slows down the aging process and doesn't stop it completely. We're all going to get old and gray one day, but I don't see anything wrong with slowing the process as much as possible. Last, as you get older, you have to make sure your finances are on point. As an older man, you can't expect to have the same sexual market value as you did when you were younger unless your finances have increased. A good way of looking at it is, as your looks deteriorate, your finances increase. Women do not have this luxury, thus they start to put more emphasis on settling down as they age. Men care very little about how much money a woman makes, which is why you'll see a great deal of women who aren't married at an older age pushing so hard for a relationship. That's because they know their best days are behind them, and they are looking to nab the highest-quality male they can with what's left of their youth and beauty. If you're a red-pill man and content with casually dating and nonmonogamous relationships, I think you have to put a lot of emphasis on creating the type of lifestyle that more than makes up for what you lack physically. As an older man, you have to be completely delusional if you want to attract women half your age when you're fifty years old and expect your financial stability not to play a major role in that attraction. Of course, as with anything, there will be outliers who can do this, but they're called outliers for a reason and shouldn't be expected to be the norm. Most men have an issue with being considered beta-male providers, but this should not be an issue when you get older. A fifty-year-old man shouldn't expect a twenty-two-year-old to be highly attracted to him physically. Of course, you still could charm her panties off, but it's just not practical to think a woman half your age once you reach fifty is only with you for just you. I know for a fact that women do not show men they perceive as beta providers the same affection and respect as they do to men they perceive as alpha males, but my rebuttal to these men with this issue would be to keep the engagements brief. If you choose to date women who perceive you as a beta male, then at the very minimum, keep it to once a week. Don't try to build anything with women who view you as a beta male because you'll always have this feeling of emptiness when dealing with them, which in turn causes you to doubt yourself and lose confidence, which then actually makes you classify yourself as a beta male. Once you deem yourself a beta male, it's hard to ever consider yourself an alpha male, as you start to accept your value to women to only be financial.

58

Signs of a Manipulative Woman

It's always nice to date women with high interest from the start. They make it very easy to date them and alleviate any nervousness when you reach out to set the next date. There are some women, however, who, beyond just exhibiting initial high interest, will go as far as to express their interest verbally or through text message. This is always a red flag to men because women are taught to play hard to get. Women are taught this because it makes men value them more. So why would some women overly express their interest level if they're taught to play hard to get? The answer is simple: manipulation. Now, some women will have a genuinely high interest, but some will purposely lure you in with extremely high cooperation. Men chase cooperation, while women chase validation. By "cooperation," I'm referring to how easy a woman makes it for you at the initial meeting. Unfortunately, you won't be able to tell which woman is which until you start to date them. I'll admit that sometimes a man can do things to lower a woman's interest, but if you've been following me for a while, I think it's safe to say you aren't doing anything to lower her interest. These are the women who will make it so easy for you initially only to pull back later. I'm not telling you to shy away from women exhibiting high interest; what I am telling you is to be on the lookout for women who purposely display high interest initially only to pull back later.

These women purposely express crazy-high initial interest only to later pull back to get you to chase them. The thing is, you're not actually chasing a woman because had she displayed that level of interest, it's very unlikely you would have pursued her, but since she made things so easy initially, you're chasing the level of initial cooperation. Highly manipulative women have several reasons for this, but commonly it's done for merely their enjoyment. Some women just get off on manipulating men because it's fun to them. I'm not saying you shouldn't date women who display high interest initially, but you should be cognizant of what might happen. Just think to yourself for a second: how many women have you dated that showed a tremendous amount of initial interest, and it stayed that way for an extended period of time? I'm well aware of it being her feeling of newness at meeting a new guy, or perhaps you no longer consider yourself an alpha, causing her interest to drop, but more often than not, it has nothing to do with you. Rather, it's just some sick thrill some women get out of playing with men's emotions. There's an old saying: "If something is too good to be true, it usually is." I think that statement is true when it comes to dating women who exhibit crazy-high initial interest. As a high-value man, you shouldn't be so easily manipulated.

59

Women Popping Up Unannounced and Nesting

Women who've made it their agenda to get you in a relationship have a couple of tricks up their sleeves to do this. Women have a way of marking their territory, so to speak. One way that women accomplish this is by popping up unannounced at your residence. They do this in the hope of having you in a state of paranoia about bringing other women to your residence, despite you making your intentions known about having an open relationship. As a high-value man, you have to have boundaries, and this definitely crosses a boundary. Even if you're in a monogamous relationship, no one should pop up announced unless the two of you are living together. If you're in a monogamous relationship, and trust is an issue, then you should let her know that a lack of trust isn't going to work. If you've cheated and have gotten caught, then you have to let her know either she's going to have to trust you again or you're better off being single. When a woman doesn't trust you, she can literally turn your life into a living hell of insecurities. While I understand where the insecurities come from, and rightfully so, I'm not about to walk on eggshells dealing with someone else's insecurities. Women also pop up unannounced to see how much they can get away with—a shit test of sorts. If you let this go unchecked, it'll only get worse from there. I wouldn't say this is a fireable offense, but it's definitely worthy of letting them know that type of behavior will not be tolerated. Women are just like anybody else in society; they test to see where the boundaries are. You have to let it be known from the start what your boundaries are.

Women also have the uncanny ability to leave behind items of theirs at your residence. This is not done by accident. This is a woman's way of marking her territory to other women who may come over to your residence. This is called nesting. You can try to remind her to make sure she doesn't leave items behind at your residence, but she'll just play coy and act as if it was an innocent mistake. Although you may have informed other women about the fact that you're only interested in an open relationship, it's still a mood killer for women to find other women's items left behind. To avoid this, you should do a house sweep when every woman leaves your residence. Sometimes a woman may think she's the only woman you're dating, although the conversation about exclusivity hasn't come up yet. To be fair, you don't owe anybody an explanation if the exclusivity talk hasn't come up yet. You're not lying to anybody, because as far as you're concerned, she's dating multiple men. Dating one person at a time is stupid and not a very effective way to find a significant other, if that's something you aspire to obtain. Until you're exclusive with a woman, it's always best to date multiple women because it offers you the best opportunity to meet a woman who is compatible with you instead of just settling for the next best thing. If the topic comes up, then you should always be open about your dating life, as it's actually a sign of having a scarcity mind-set to lie to women about your dating life. A man should have the mind-set that either she's down with who you are or she's not; why do you think women are so open about their children on their dating profiles or when you first meet them? That's because women are of the mind-set that if a man can't handle them having kids, then he can go kick rocks.

Men should have this same kind of mind-set. Never lie about your finances, income, and so on to get laid. It's not because you're a man of morals; it's because you're a man with an abundance mind-set that says, "Accept me for who I am." You must understand that once you become a high-value man, you control the pace at which the relationship progresses after the initial meeting. Women control the pace initially because they are the gatekeepers for sex, but high-value men control the pace of the relationship.

60

Women You Should Not Take Back

I teach men to leave women when they become disrespectful and to only take them back if they're willing to make it up to the men. This could be them cooking for you, cleaning your place, and so on. It doesn't always have to be something sexual. It's key that a man makes a woman prove herself before taking her back because you don't want women feeling like they can come in and go out of your life whenever they get ready. I know you're probably thinking, "I broke up with her," but I beg to differ. Women are passive-aggressive, and when they want out of a relationship, they're notorious for pushing men away with bad behavior. Despite this intolerable behavior, some men still don't have the balls to leave the relationship due to their scarcity mind-set. If you are one of the few men who actually has the balls to leave the relationship, there are a few situations where I advise you to do so.

If you catch a woman cheating, you must leave that relationship. Women are way more thoughtful than men, and the fact that she even got caught is indicative of her respect level for you. Women cheat primarily for one of a few reasons. Either she's not getting the emotional support from home, she's not being satisfied sexually at home, she perceives you as a beta male, or she views you as an alpha male and the relationship has lost all of its sexual tension. I'm not saying that if a woman views you as a beta male that she's automatically going to cheat, but if the opportunity presents itself, she will, more than likely. When I'm referring to the opportunity presenting itself, I'm referring to meeting a man she perceives as an alpha male and him understanding how to play his role, which is that he understands that this is strictly a sexual relationship and nothing more. It's better if she's cheating for sexual desire than for emotional reasons because if she's cheating for emotional reasons, it means she's bonded with the other guy, and you're basically her beta-male provider at that point; nonetheless, either situation is not ideal. This is one of the many reasons you shouldn't even consider engaging in anything long term or serious with a woman who views you as a beta-male provider. She's way more likely to cheat to get that sexual desire met. Although it may be better if a woman is cheating for sexual desire rather than for emotional support, I would still advise against taking a woman back who's been caught cheating no matter the reason. The primary reason is that as a high-value male, you have goals in life you're trying to obtain; how are you supposed to conquer the world if you're wondering what your girl is doing? You'll live in a state of constant paranoia. Here's the catch, though; despite her being the one who caused your insecurities, she'll start to lose attraction due to your insecurities. Isn't that something? Save yourself the headache, and just let her go. It also stands to reason: how much respect do you think she'll have for a man who takes a woman back who got caught cheating? This is like the Mount Rushmore of scarcity mind-sets.

You should also never get back with a woman who's caught you cheating. I often refer to men who get caught cheating as the world's biggest cockblockers, so I think it's a simp move if you cheat in a monogamous relationship. That aside, if you do, however, cheat and get caught, I think it's a bad idea to get back with that woman. Women can be vindictive, and you'll always be looking over your shoulder, waiting for her to get back at you. You must also consider the aspect that she'll most likely never trust you again. Her not trusting you again presents another problem in itself. If she doesn't trust you, then it stands to reason that she'll never give herself to you completely. In other words, she'll hold back. When a woman holds back, you can expect it to feel like you're alone even though you're in a relationship.

You should never take a woman back who hit you or made any kind of physical contact. The reason for this is simple: as a high-value man, you're not going to risk your career and freedom for some overly emotional woman who's incapable of keeping her hands to herself. Dealing with these kinds of women puts you in a position to defend yourself in a society where men aren't allowed to defend themselves. Don't get me wrong; I don't think a man should hit a woman, but it's not because you shouldn't be allowed to defend yourself. I believe you shouldn't hit a woman because you should've left that toxic relationship long ago. Toxic relationships where the woman is hitting the man aren't an overnight situation. These relationships have been toxic for a very long time. As a high-value man, you should've left long ago. If a woman hits you, it's because she's lost all respect for you. When I'm referring to her loss of respect, I'm referring to you not having the strength to leave her despite her unruly behavior for months, if not longer. That loss of respect has culminated in her resorting to violence. Even if you didn't have the strength to leave, you must understand that this woman's interest is at rock bottom and under no circumstances should you ever consider taking her back. The reason for this, other than the obvious, is that once a woman gets physical with you, it's highly likely she will again in the future. Some women actually take advantage of how men are incapable of defending themselves and use it to their benefit. You don't want to have a woman who's purposely trying to provoke you into an altercation.

The final situation where a man shouldn't take a woman back is when he catches her invading his privacy. This can be going through his phone, rambling through his closet, and so on. The reason for this is simple: you must trust your woman. You shouldn't fear leaving your woman in your home while you run an errand. I know that it's female nature to snoop around, but men should never tolerate this type of behavior. If it was something you wanted her to know, then you would have told her about it. That's an invasion of privacy, and if you catch it, you should end that relationship immediately.

61

Staying in a Relationship for the Kids

A lot of men with kids claim that despite having a woman who's out of control, they're going to stay in the relationship for the kids. I understand some men want to be around their children growing up, as family court is very unfair to men as far as custody goes. So what I get is a lot of questions about how to get a woman to respect them without leaving her. That's like asking me how to get rich without working. You can have your cake and eat it too. Relationships are about leverage, and being married with kids gives the woman leverage in the relationship. A man has the leverage when the woman knows he'll leave if she's uncooperative. I know a lot of people will read that last statement and think, "Relationships are not about leverage, but rather love and commitment." Pretty much every aspect of your life is about leverage, if you think about it. How much you get paid at your job is based on how in demand you are. If you have several companies vying for your services, then you're way more likely to get a better salary than if you don't. If you have several friends you can call on, then all of your friends would undoubtedly treat you better since you have no scarcity of friends. If you run a business, and you have hundreds of customers, you're not going to tolerate unruly patrons as you would if you only had a few customers. I saw this firsthand at a gym I worked at in Manhattan. A potential new member of the gym tried to negotiate a better deal for their membership, and the member advisor told them right there on the spot that they didn't negotiate prices. In other words, "Here's our price. Either you want it, or you don't." Abundance creates respect from your peers and, more importantly, your woman. Children or not, the only way a man can maintain leverage and respect in a relationship is that the woman has to know he has no problem leaving the relationship. If a woman has the leverage, she loses attraction for the man because at that point, she has the power in the relationship. Despite feminism being so prevalent in today's society, women still subconsciously want a man that can lead. I hate to say this, but it has to be said. Let's be honest, most of you not leaving really doesn't have that much to do with the kids. It's mostly about you and your scarcity mind-set. In reality, you're using the children as a scapegoat as to why you're unable to leave. The fact of the matter is, every man needs to show his woman he's willing to leave if she isn't cooperating. I don't have children, but I'm well aware and familiar with acquiring assets with a woman. These assets could be a home or car you may have purchased together. It is as if you are giving up the large chunk of your life that it took to acquire those assets, but I would counter that assertion: what's your self-respect and peace of mind worth? So while I understand your dilemma, the facts remain the same. For the few men who actually are staying in these toxic relationships, you would actually be doing your children more harm than good. While ideally a two-parent home is better, you must understand that only applies if it's a loving relationship. Well, it doesn't have to be exactly loving but at least not toxic. How much good do you think you're doing your kids if Mom and Dad are bickering all the time? They'll grow up thinking that this is normal. If you have sons, they'll grow up beta, thinking it's normal for the woman to wear the pants, and if you have a daughter, she'll grow up masculine, thinking women are supposed to run the household. Coincidentally, this is why you have so many men letting women run the relationship while these men stay feeling emasculated. Women don't respect words; they only respect action. You not leaving shows her you have no sexual market value, thus why you're afraid to leave. This kills her attraction to you, since she figures you can't get anyone else, and that's why you take her crap. Acting more masculine won't put her back in her feminine energy. The only thing that will get her back into her feminine energy is for you to raise her attraction level back up. And the only thing that can raise her attraction level back up is to show her you have options. A man's options are directly linked to preselection. If you decide to stay in the relationship, you must understand that the best you'll be able to do is get her to respect you. I highly doubt you'll be able to get the passion back into the relationship. I'm a firm believer that once that's gone, it never comes back. Maybe the passion never comes back, but if you have her respect, at least she won't be a headache. Preselection is always king with attraction. It's another form of status. As a man, you always have to work to improve your sexual market value so your woman knows you have other options. A woman only respects a man if he has options. You might've noticed a common theme. Men have to leave toxic, disrespectful relationships. If you're wondering why I mention it so much, it is because I'm assuming that if you're reading this book, your woman is probably being a pain in the butt. Men are trying to figure out how to get their woman to respect them without doing what needs to be done. It kind of reminds me of how overweight people try to find ways to lose weight other than diet and exercise. It's hard for a reason, but little gimmicks don't work. Respect is earned, not given. Assertiveness is something women find very attractive. Being assertive is achieved when you're able to express your point or convey your message without getting overly aggressive and emotional. The only way you can be assertive is if a woman knows there are consequences behind your words. Speak softly and carry a big stick.

62

You Must Have Game

The word "game" is derived from the phrase "game plan." To attract a woman, you need a game plan. To sleep with a woman, you need a game plan. To get a woman to want a relationship—for men who actually desire a wife—you need to have a game plan to entice the woman to marry you. The game plan you use to entice a woman is going to vary from woman to woman. Football teams don't use the same game plan for every football game, and you won't be able to use the same game plan for every woman. A game plan isn't something you have to sit around and actually plan out. High-value men's game plan is to simply be themselves. A high-value man is busy and unavailable. Now this just so happens to raise the interest level of a lot of women, but it's not like it's you trying to do this. Only fake high-value men have to act busy. You should be busy. But being busy and unavailable won't do it all by itself. You actually have to have a personality that she likes. A lot of men confuse charisma with game, but I think there is a distinct difference. Your personality is different from game in the respect that your personality is your personality. You can't strategize that. Either she likes the words that are coming out, or she doesn't. There is no right or wrong personality. It really just boils down to taste. The only personality that is universally disliked is an insecure personality. Other than that, everything else is a matter of preference. But let's put that aside; there are different paths you can take to attract and raise the interest of the women you desire. Understand the best path is to become the best version of yourself and to develop an abundance mind-set. No matter how corny you may think you are, somewhere there is a woman who would love to share your company. So you must understand that only low-value men with a scarcity mind-set use a designed game plan to attract women; high-value men simply just are themselves, and even when they meet women who don't like them for who they are, these men have the abundance mind-set to keep it moving. The strategies I'm about to lay out shouldn't really be strategies at all but rather, if you've been paying attention to this book, a lifestyle. To low-value men who don't want to do self-improvement, then admittedly they are strategies. A lot of men fail with women because they try to use the same game plan for every woman. When a woman is looking for a relationship, I can all but guarantee you she'll lose interest if you try to reach out once a week to set a date. Women who are seeking relationships tend to pursue, if you're a man they can see themselves with in a relationship, to move things along, so to speak. If you don't reciprocate her pursuit, she'll just assume you aren't looking for the same thing she is looking for and move on. If you don't care about adjusting, then that's your choice, but just understand you'll be losing out on a lot of female companionship, if you know what I mean. If you're a high-value man with limited time, I understand you may not have an hour in your day to chat on the phone, but a simple good-morning text goes a long way here. It doesn't take a whole lot. As I've mentioned before, a lot of men have taken my high-value lifestyle way out of context. Just because you're high-value doesn't mean you have time for a simple text if the woman is showing genuine interest. Just make sure you let these women know you like to take your time and not to rush into things. Ironically a woman who's just enjoying her single life loses attraction when a man comes across too strong by reaching out more than once a week to set a date. No woman is attracted to a man who's actively seeking a relationship, even if the woman prefers a relationship. She might initially have attraction, but it'll die quickly because a man who's looking for a relationship comes across subconsciously as a man without many options. Women want to feel like they had to win you over from all your many options of women. The way to avoid this is by not overpursuing. This can be done accidentally because you fall into the trap of her pursuing, so you might have a tendency to overdo it. There's a fine line between underpursuing and overpursuing. I accept the risk of leaving a lot of female companionship on the table because at this point, sleeping with as many women as I possibly can is no longer my focus. I'm more concerned with my purpose in life than to worry about sleeping with a wide variety of women anymore, and that's what being high value is truly about. The God's honest truth is, if your main goal is to sleep with as many women as you possibly can, the best method to accomplish that is to play the numbers game all day every day. The numbers game is when you approach as many women as you possibly can on any given day and hope you meet some women who like you. Being a high-value man will never be the best method to sleep with the most women. You simply don't spend enough time pursuing women. Being high value is about losing your addiction to women. Being high value is about no longer letting your little head allow you to be manipulated by women. Just understand I'm writing this book for the sole purpose of helping not just my red-pill brothers but also my purple-pill brothers who accept female nature for what it is and choose to engage in a monogamous relationship. I'm not here to judge anyone, as I'm a firm believer in different strokes for different folks. By default, if you're familiar with my work and teachings, you're automatically purple or red pill. There's no way you can be familiar with my work and consider yourself blue pill. Charisma is subjective, but if you're dating a woman whom charisma-wise you just don't do it for, you still have a card you can play. You can just shut the hell up! For men who think they have no charisma, you must understand that you don't need charisma. If the woman finds you attractive, the strong, silent type has been and always will be attractive to a lot of women so long as you can at least hold a decent conversation. A woman could find you attractive, but if you lack the charisma that she likes to go along with it, then she could lose attraction very quickly. It's not that you lack charisma, but maybe you lack the charisma she's accustomed to. You could always just be silent. Silence is synonymous with being mysterious. Of course, you can't be a mute, but by and large, women find mysterious men attractive so long as these men know what to say when the time comes. The thing with being mysterious is, it only works if a woman finds you attractive. If a woman doesn't find you that attractive, being the strong, silent type won't do much in the way of raising her interest. If a woman doesn't find you very attractive, you're going to need to raise her attraction with your charisma. If charisma-wise you're not compatible, then it simply won't work, unless she's looking for a provider and you have your life in order. The rules go as follows: if a woman finds you attractive, then you don't need compatible charisma so long as you remain mysterious. If a woman doesn't find you that attractive, then you're going to have to be compatible in terms of charisma because that's the only way you can raise her interest to sleep with her, unless she's looking for a provider and you have your stuff together. If you're trying to use women's hypergamous nature against them, you have to have a game plan because women are notorious for using men whom they have no sexual desires for. I really shouldn't refer to it as a game plan, because it's actually more about rules you should follow when dealing with a woman who perceives you as a beta male. This is why it's so important to keep the cost of your dates down initially and to stick to the three-date rule. Sticking to those principles prevents you from getting played. Women who are materialistic have a game plan, and it usually revolves around using a man's sexual desires against him. They do this by dressing in sexy clothes to manipulate as many resources as they can without sleeping with you. Some women will actually sleep with you and then pull back, so you chase her with your wallet in the hope of sleeping with her again. If you're the type to use a woman's hypergamous nature against her, you should just keep in mind that these are the kinds of women who have the most game, so you have to be on point. The best thing that a man who's trying to use a woman's nature against her can do is to have a firm timeline for sex to happen. If you don't, you can find yourself in a hamster wheel, chasing sex from her for years.

63

Standing Up to Haters When You're with Your Girl

Men are supposed to be protectors of the household. If you have an attractive woman, you can expect men to cross boundaries when you're with your woman. Attractiveness is in the eye of the beholder, so even if you consider your woman average, she might be a dime to someone else, which won't exclude you from haters' negativity. A great way to negate a physical or verbal confrontation with haters is to hold a strong masculine frame when you're with your girl. Actually, you should hold a masculine frame all the time. Holding a masculine frame might negate some negativity when you're out and about with your woman, but it won't stop it entirely. Men love discussing women's nature but don't spend any time discussing male nature, which is mainly jealousy. When you're with your woman, the only reason men try to disrespect you is their jealousy. They're basically trying to emasculate you in front of your girl. If that woman was out and about by herself, they probably wouldn't even say anything to her. Avoiding certain locations that are known for drawing the wrong crowd might help, but quite frankly, you could be at a restaurant when some asshole disrespects you. So how should you respond if someone does? Well, this is one of those situations where it just depends on how much your self-respect matters to you. If it's me, I'm standing up for myself every time. Could the guy have a weapon? Most certainly he could, but as a man, my self-respect matters more to me than anything. I can assure you right now that if you don't stand up for yourself, there will be a lot of sleepless nights. Being emasculated can have an everlasting effect. Years can pass, and you could possibly still be living with that shame. If you don't stand up for yourself, you should expect your woman to lose a little respect for you. This is mainly due to her not feeling safe when she's with you. Men are expected to be providers and protectors. There's a difference between standing up for yourself and acting insecure. A man looking at your woman is not a reason to check a man. Let them look; that's what you should expect if you think highly of your woman. I damn sure don't want a woman who never turns heads. I generally wait until I hear something disrespectful before I react. Some men are so brazen that they'll even go as far as to grab your woman. This is obviously a rare situation, but it does happen. Never resort to violence unless it's in self-defense. You have to learn how to stand up for yourself without initiating physical contact. You can simply say something like, "Hey, dude. Don't disrespect me and my girl like that." A response like that should usually do the trick because most of these individuals who engage in that type of behavior are cowards. Cowards usually try to find individuals they perceive as weaker to pick on. This makes them feel better about themselves. Be warned that some of these individuals might escalate the situation. If it's me, I only resort to violence to defend myself. So if they make you feel threatened, you have every human right to defend yourself.

64

When to Buy Women Gifts and What to Get

E very man who's in a relationship is always confused as to what to get his woman for her birthday or Christmas. You can buy a woman gifts for Valentine's if you prefer, but for Valentine's Day, I prefer to do something romantic like dinner and a bubble bath. If you're in a nonmonogamous relationship, you're probably wondering if you should get her anything at all. Well, if that's your scenario, then it depends on a host of variables. Those variables include, but are not limited to, the amount of time the two of you have been dating, whether she is buying you something, and her interest level, which is directly correlated to her cooperation. I'm not buying an uncooperative woman—that is, a low-interest woman— anything, regardless of how long we've been dating. Quite frankly, at this point in my life, I don't care how good the sex is; to me, an uncooperative woman and I won't be dating very long at all. For hard-core red-pill men who don't believe in buying women gifts, then you must understand that every woman wants to feel appreciated from time to time. Now, if you're a pump-and-dump kind of guy, then this book really isn't for you at all. I'm writing this book more for men who like rotations and men who are in relationships, whether it's monogamous or nonmonogamous. I consider a rotation to be dating the same women, not a constant revolving door. Sleeping with women is nothing; it's actually more work to maintain the attention of several women. Men take everything to the extreme. Men tend to be either beta simps or Ike Turner hard. As I've mentioned before, balance is the key. I don't see anything wrong with buying women gifts for their birthday or Christmas, but I do see something wrong with buying women random gifts for no reason at all. Essentially, you're putting her on a pedestal and subconsciously conveying to her that this is what you have to do to keep her happy. You alone should be enough to keep her happy. A universal gift I've found to always work is a purse or bag. The brand of this purse depends on what brand your woman prefers. You can find this out by simply paying attention to what brands she carries when you're with her. If it's a brand that's not in your budget, then try to get a brand that's classy and plain. You generally can't go wrong with a plain purse. Remember, it's the thought that counts, but don't be a cheapskate either. Another good gift I've observed that works is high heels. The same rules apply here, as I recommend getting a brand she wears often. In both situations, you want to make sure it's a style she doesn't already have. Although it's the thought that counts, you want to make sure it's a brand she likes because if it is, then she's more likely to wear it. Nobody likes to buy someone something that they never use or wear.

65

Why I'm So against the Direct Approach

I've gotten some flak from some men who don't like my stance on the direct approach. The biggest issue I have with using a direct approach is that it's outdated. We live in a different world than we did when this tactic was first introduced. We live in a world where everything a man does is considered sexual harassment. I mean, if you look at a woman wrong, it's sexual harassment; how are you supposed to openly talk sexually to a woman then? I think it's irresponsible for anyone to teach young men, or old men for that matter, to use this technique when it can get them fired from their job, expelled from school, or get charged with sexual harassment. I understand that it's not all sexual talk, but if someone misuses this technique, it can have lasting consequences on their career and livelihood. I wrote about this in my first book, but I feel so passionate about this that I felt compelled to discuss it again, as it's not only a poor technique to use but also an irresponsible one. Men who teach a direct approach show you that their more direct approach is just like anything else when a man is trying to obtain sex from women, and that's a strategy, and just like every other strategy, it's going to work on some women, while on others it won't. The only women this approach is going to work on is the women who view you as an alpha male or the women with very high initial interest. That alone lets you know this is more of a gimmick than an actual strategy. I would guess that 90 to 95 percent of the women who view you are going to have an average to low initial interest level. That means that you'll only be able to sleep with 5 percent of the women you meet. That's a very low percentage. Even a novice could sleep with 20 percent of the women he meets. When I was in the fitness industry, you see a lot of lose-weight-fast gimmicks and gadgets, and that's exactly what using a direct approach with a woman you've just met is: a gimmick. I understand that using a direct approach is about not letting women take advantage of you. It also suggests that women are as visual as men. Be this as it may, I still say it's a flawed strategy because women are not as visual as men. Looks do matter to women, so I don't want to cast that illusion that they don't matter, but they don't matter nearly as much as they do to men. When you use a direct approach, you lose a man's greatest asset, and that's the ability to raise a woman's interest with your personality, confidence, and strength. If you don't remember anything else that I tell you, just remember this one saying: "Everyone wants something out the deal." Men have sex because we want a sexual release. Women have sex to have a sexual release also, but most women can't cum during sex unless they have direct clitoral stimulation, so most women accept the fact that they won't get the same enjoyment from sex as men do. Another way women can cum is when they're emotionally attached to you, but you can't expect a woman to get emotionally attached to you upon the initial meeting, so it stands to reason that the woman won't get anything out of it sexually initially unless you indulge in oral sex, which is never a good idea with a woman you just met. Now just ask yourself this: what's in it for her? Women sleep with men on the first night for one of (or a combination of any of) the following reasons. You have status, she finds you extremely attractive and you didn't talk yourself out of it, or you pay for it, either directly or indirectly. The average man just isn't going to have the status or sex appeal to sleep with women on the first night. I don't even respect men who pay women for sex. In a normal setting, the trade for a man and woman is sexual attention for nonsexual attention. This is, of course, if she puts a value on your nonsexual attention. Another reason would be sexual attention for monetary gain. This monetary gain could come in the form of money directly, gifts, dates, or being a beta-male provider in a relationship. The reason guys want to make the direct approach a mainstay in dating is that it does the same thing get-rich-quick schemes and fast-weight-loss programs offer, and that's quick results with minimal effort. It's much easier to go up to random women trying to obtain sex, all the while proclaiming a direct approach. Raising a woman's interest is work, and most men just want to take the easy way out. Don't get me wrong; as a high-value man, you shouldn't be trying to raise a woman's interest that is too low, but on the same token, you don't want to lose an opportunity with women you have a legitimate chance with. As I've mentioned earlier, men tend to go to extremes when dating. Using a direct approach is an extreme, and trying to raise the interest level of women with very low interest is an extreme. Using a direct approach is ineffective in most situations because it takes the stance that women are like men and mostly physical, which is false. The old saying "Men fall in love through their eyes, while women fall in love through their ears" has a lot of truth to it. I have slept with women on the first night, but it had very little to do with me. It had more to do with the woman's high initial interest, and I couldn't screw it up if I wanted to. As the years go by, there will always be some weirdos who come along and try to reinvent the wheel to obtain a buck from men. These men are no better than the women who use men's sexual desires against them for financial gain. Self-improvement will always give a man his best chance at attracting women, not silly gimmicks.

To be fair, I do believe there's a time and place for using a direct approach. If you're a man in a monogamous relationship and don't want to get caught, a direct approach would probably work best because there's a very good chance you won't have the disposable time to raise a woman's interest. I'm not condoning cheating behavior, but if you're going to do it, at least be proficient at it. The reason I'm against a man cheating has nothing to do with morality. If you wanted to sleep with other women, then why not just stay a bachelor? The reason is simple: scarcity. I also refer to men who cheat as the world's biggest cockblockers. The reason I use this term is that men knowingly get into monogamous relationships to prevent the woman they're in a relationship with from sleeping with other men. They want to have their cake and eat it too. Instead of just dating the woman, which would undoubtedly leave the woman available to sleep with other men, you took the coward's route and made a commitment just to prevent her from sleeping with other men, despite that not being what you truly wanted to do.

Another great time to use a direct approach is when you're on vacation. When you're on vacation, there's a very good chance you won't have time to raise a woman's interest, so you have nothing to lose by using a more direct approach. However, if you have time to raise her interest, essentially having a direct approach is a lack of confidence in your game. Basically you're saying, "I have no confidence in my ability to raise your interest with my game and charm, so I need to know right now if you have enough physical attraction to me to sleep with me, or else I'll just be wasting my time." Game, in a nutshell, is your strategy to raise a woman's interest so she'll feel attracted to you. Understand, however, that even in those situations, you run the risk of getting charged with sexual harassment if you approach the wrong female.

Getting into a Relationship with a Woman You Took from Another Guy

All is fair in love and war. That saying simply means it's every man for himself. When women start losing interest in a man they're dating or in a relationship, they'll usually start to pull back before the relationship ends. During this pullback, the woman may start dating other men or, at the very minimum, start giving out her contact information. While I don't think it's right to date a married woman, I see nothing wrong with dating a woman who's just in a relationship, but to be honest, it's all the same. Just be aware of the little thing called karma if you decide to go that route. When a woman wants to cheat but keeps her beta-male provider at home, she'll usually inform you of the situation so you know how to play your position. If a woman is ready to move on, it's likely she won't even tell you she's involved. Generally speaking, you should be able to tell if you're dating a woman who's in a relationship just by her patterns of behavior. She'll be very inconsistent in her behavior, and you won't be able to get ahold of her for hours on end. There are some women who go the extra mile to avoid getting caught, so in those situations, you may never know if a woman is in a relationship with someone else unless she tells you or they're living together. The reason for this is that's just how women move on. Guys must understand that a lot of what I teach I just got from my observations of how women behave. I don't want men acting like women, but I do want men to develop the abundance mindset that women have. When women go out, they aren't looking to pick up men from the club. They're there to just enjoy themselves. I'm trying to get men to adopt that same mind-set. Women keep men in the friend zone to serve their self-serving needs of constant validation and, in some cases, to have as a backup plan. I teach men to keep women in the friend zone for the same reasons. I know a lot of men won't like that last statement because they have oneitis and fear other men sleeping with their woman, but men have to start seeing the world for how it is and not for how they want to see it. These are the same men who are confused as to how their woman just lost attraction all of a sudden, but if they had been paying attention, they would've noticed she had been pulling back for weeks, if not months. Who knows? Maybe you took another man's girl and just didn't know. Women are rarely ever completely single, so there's a very good chance when you started dating her that she was involved with someone else and pulled back to be with you. If you knowingly start dating a woman in a relationship, and the relationship grows to where she's pushing for a relationship with you, I would advise against getting into a monogamous relationship with these kinds of women. I'm a big proponent of the law of attraction, and therefore karma will eventually come back to bite you in the behind big time. You'll be the one on the heartbreak side this time. I've dated women in relationships, but the difference is that I never get attached; therefore, I'm not afraid of karma coming back at me. If you're a hard-core red-pill guy, then you don't have this concern, but if you're a purple-pill guy, you should keep these women off-limits for a relationship. These kinds of women don't have the decency to end things with you before moving on.

CHAPTER

67

It's Her Frame of Mind, Not Her Interest Level

Occasionally you may encounter a woman who just does it for you in every way, but despite her obvious high interest level, things don't seem to be progressing the way you think they should. While I don't believe anyone should be looking for a relationship, there will come a time, if you're a purple-pill guy, when you're dating a woman and may want things to be a little more exclusive once you've caught feelings, so to speak. One of the reasons she might be avoiding exclusivity is women can sense when a man is more into them than they are into him. When a woman senses this, it lowers her attraction because the challenge of obtaining his validation is gone. Just keep in mind that the relationship always moves at the woman's pace. So if things aren't progressing, it's because she doesn't want things to progress. The reason she isn't pursuing you more or asking to see you more is that she's not in the mind-set of having anything more than just casual sex or dating without a commitment, which usually means she's dating other men; however, that may not always be the case. She could just be enjoying her freedom as a single woman, or she literally might be sleeping with five or six other dudes. It's virtually impossible to raise a woman's interest to the level where she wants more exclusivity until she's in the right frame of mind for more exclusivity. You could be doing everything right, and she still won't pursue more because she's enjoying her freedom. I know this because there's nothing a woman could do to make me want a relationship right now, no matter how sexy or feminine she is. I'm not looking for anything more than casual dating at the moment, so my guard is up, so to speak. By my guard being up, I'm simply referring to the fact that I take all preventive measures against getting attached, like seeing a woman no more than twice a week, preferably once, never dating just one woman at a time, and never giving a woman lots of my nonsexual attention. When a woman has her guard up, you'll see some of these similar things. This is not by accident; she's deliberately holding back to prevent getting attached. When someone's guard is up, only they can take it down. Them letting their guard down has more to do with them being tired of the game than with their interest in you. In other words, when they're tired of juggling multiple people or want something more meaningful, then they'll be open to the possibility of a relationship. As with anything in life, it's mostly timing. A woman could be with a man for ten years, and the man could be unwillingly to marry her. She decides to finally move on, or they just break up because the relationship ran its course, and low and behold, six months later, he's married. Now, this could just be a case of the man not thinking the previous woman was marriage material, but sometimes it could just be a case of the man maturing with time. Another thing to consider in those types of situations is the man might've learned from his previous experience of losing one good woman, and now he has cold feet and doesn't want it to happen again. Women can enjoy dating more than men due to their wide variety of choices, whereas most men simply don't have as many options to date as many women as women do with men. When women go through what most of us men refer to in the manosphere as the "slut phase," there's nothing you can do to make her want to progress things. You need to accept that, or she's going to start feeling your energy and feel you want more than she's willing to give at the moment. A man should never try to progress things because it's an attraction killer to women.

CHAPTER

68

Women Don't Respect Apologies

firmly believe that a man should never apologize to a woman. Not only do most women consider this a sign of weakness, but women are notorious for playing the victim. They do this by crying in the midst of an argument to draw sympathy from a man, even when they're in the wrong. In giving this sympathy, a man would usually apologize to the woman. In doing so, the man has just shown the woman how to manipulate him. Start an argument, drop a few tears, and voilà, the man starts to apologize. Now understand that I'm taking this from the perspective that the man hasn't done anything wrong. If you've forgotten your anniversary, got caught cheating, or called your woman out her name, then, yes, apologize. I'm taking the perspective that your woman has taken some minuscule disagreement and turned it into this big disagreement. This is then followed by tears to draw sympathy. So what started out as a disagreement over where to vacation this year has turned into this big, blowout fight and her crying. If you apologize because you had an opinion on this issue, you can expect this same behavior next time this kind of discussion comes around. Some men are familiar with women's manipulation, but a lot of men don't understand why women use manipulation tactics like crying in the midst of an argument. The answer is quite simple, however: it's to get their way. Men are blessed with more strength and drive due to testosterone, which on a level playing field inhibits women from competing from a physical standpoint, but from a psychological standpoint, women are far ahead of men because they're master manipulators. The funny thing is that women aren't attracted to men they can manipulate. Letting a woman manipulate you is a sign of weakness and scarcity. If you're in the mind-set of abundance, and a woman tries to run her manipulation, it won't work because you have no fear of loss. Manipulation tactics only work if you fear losing the woman. The manipulation tactics are to make you afraid of losing her, which causes you to chase or apologize unnecessarily. In other words, women only try to manipulate men who they perceive as beta males. A woman instinctively knows she can't manipulate a man she perceives as an alpha male because he's in the mind-set of abundance. A high-value man would never let a woman manipulate him because if things aren't progressing or going according to his program, he's out. When a woman puts a man in the friend zone, she's essentially using the man for attention and validation by manipulating the man's sexual desires.

That is why a woman can't sleep with a man who's in her friend zone. She doesn't respect you because you're too easily manipulated and in obvious scarcity. Now, you do have different friend zones a woman could put you in. There's the friend zone where you have a chance, and you're the guy on standby. You're the guy she's going to run to in the event her current situation goes south. You can tell if you're in this position because she may or may not go out with you but won't sleep with you. Her behavior may also be very inconsistent.

There's also the friend zone where you have no chance unless you increase your status, and you're relegated to being her gay male girlfriend. You can increase your status by making more money (financial status), dating more attractive women (sexual market value), and being more popular (social status).

In any case, either one of these situations is ideal, as you never know how long that standby, friend-zone position can last, and it takes time to raise your status. Men with options don't have time to be friends with a woman in the hope of gaining sex. If you're one of these men in a relationship with a woman, and she pulls out the old crying-tears bull crap, you're not in a scarcity mind-set, so the thought of her getting upset and leaving doesn't concern you one bit. For the genuine nice guys out there, being a nice guy and a pushover are two different things. Being nice is holding doors open for old people and saying thank you to people who just did you a service. Being nice has nothing to do with being easily manipulated by a woman or being taken advantage of by others. If you want to maintain the attraction of a woman, you need to make sure she keeps respecting you. A woman can't respect a man whom she's easily able to manipulate. Don't confuse respect with appreciation. A woman appreciates the men in her friend zone, but this doesn't necessarily mean she respects them. I appreciated my auntie letting me and my brother getting away with murder, but I respected my uncle more because he was strict. So a woman would undoubtedly appreciate you apologizing and letting her have her way, but that doesn't mean she'll respect you.

It's All Tricking

I've heard throughout my life from a variety of men that dating women is just another form of tricking or prostitution. Men who say this are men who are trying to feel better about themselves paying for sex. These men fail to realize that once you've become a high-value man, sex is more about the accomplishment than it is about sexual release. In other words, sex feels better when you've earned it, rather than just have it. This is why men rarely get into relationships with women they have sex with right away. Yeah, a man might appreciate the easy sex, but it just doesn't have the same value as it does with a woman who made you wait three or four dates. In that respect, men are a walking contradiction, just like women. We love when women give us sex easily, but then we usually lose attraction right away. This is the same scenario as when a woman loves when a man compliments her and just openly gives his validation away, but when you do, she loses interest. I guess you can say both sexes don't know what they want. When you're having sex with a woman you have a high attraction to for the very first time, there's this feeling of victory that comes over you. That feeling of victory comes from having to "play your cards right," so to speak, to sleep with her. Having sex with a woman who you have a high attraction to and actually made you earn it feels like We all know how complicated women can be at times, and there are no sure things when it comes to women. They lose interest at the drop of a hat. A woman could be all over you on the first date and flaking on the third date. I think every man who's dealt with his fair share of women can attest to losing some women who had crazy-high initial interest, so when you do get to sleep with a woman for the first time, there's this sense of accomplishment. I don't care what any man says; when a woman makes you wait a little longer, it feels even better. That's because she made you work for it. As humans, we all appreciate things more when we have to wait for them. While I do believe we appreciate things more if we have to wait or work for them, my timeline with sex is always three dates. I'm willing to go one more date if I think I was close to sealing the deal on the third date. That has more to do with me trying to avoid dating a woman who's using me for my time and validation. Where does the sense of accomplishment come from when you pay for sex? I mentioned earlier how I also like female companionship. I like spending time with females. The old saying is "You don't pay a prostitute for sex. You pay her to leave." That saying implies that these sorts of men don't like female companionship. My response to that would be "Then who do you like spending time with? Men?" Of course, I know married men or men in monogamous relationships pay prostitutes for the convenience of not having to spend time with them and to avoid getting caught, but there are a lot of men who are single who practice this same philosophy. The reason single men don't like female companionship is that they don't know how to handle women. I'll be the first to admit that women can be a handful if you don't know how to handle them. Men simply don't know how to make women behave. A strong masculine frame and consequences for her actions are always the remedy for female behavior. I also have to mention this: women who sell their bodies disgust me. A lot of women who sell their bodies just come across to me as having bad hygiene, or at least that's how it comes across in the movies. Proper female hygiene is of utmost importance to me, and just the thought of sleeping with a woman with bad hygiene leaves a bad taste in my mouth.

70

Overcoming Insecurities

I teach men to follow their purpose to obtain the lifestyle they want. This has more to do with filling that void we all have as opposed to just making more money, but making more money is usually a by-product of getting on your purpose, so we'll take it. Making more money usually provides men with more confidence because the average man subconsciously knows women love security to some degree, but making more money doesn't compensate for insecurities. Some men have a hard time obtaining confidence despite making more money or getting into better shape physically. This is mainly due to some underlying insecurities. A man can have insecurities about his finances or body, but those are insecurities that he can control. You can get a skill to make more money, or you can hit the gym to lose weight, but how about the insecurities you can't control, like a thinning hairline, being short, or having a crooked nose? To be fair, you could get your thinning hairline or crooked nose fixed with cosmetic surgery, but let's just assume cosmetic surgery isn't something you're willing to do or can afford at the moment. So how is a man with insecurities about himself supposed to genuinely feel confident? The answer is to learn to accept your insecurities. You must understand that no one is perfect; we all have flaws we wish we could change. Look at how many women today are having cosmetic surgeries. Cosmetic surgery used to be something only wealthy people could afford, but not any longer. Pretty much every Instagram model or stripper has had some kind of cosmetic surgery done. This is because cosmetic surgery has become so affordable now. Women having cosmetic surgery is showing you all the insecurities they've always had but couldn't do anything about until now. I don't speak very articulately, and I have a receding hairline that caused me to go bald at an early age. It never affected me because I knew everyone has something they were dealing with and not just me. Women might assume you have an insecurity about something and test your confidence with some simple trolling. If you don't respond negatively to her trolling, then she'll just leave it alone because she notices that through trolling, her assumption was incorrect. This doesn't just apply to women; this also applies to people in general. They'll test you, but if you handle it correctly, they'll just leave it alone. You handle trolling by not getting overly emotional and trolling back in a nondefensive way. Whenever you want to bitch and complain about small, insignificant insecurities, just keep in mind there are people who would trade places with you in a heartbeat. You may be short due to your mom and pop's genetics, but there's always someone who's short due to not having legs. Sometimes we get so caught up in worrying about what we don't have that we forget to be thankful for what we do have. No amount of self-improvement will cover for your insecurities. The only remedy is to accept your flaws and just know everyone has them.

CHAPTER

71

Respect over Perception

Confirming dates has long been considered something that high-value men shouldn't do. It makes you look like a guy who's accustomed to women flaking on him. Unfortunately, today we live in the social media age where it's more difficult than ever to maintain a woman's interest. Thanks to social media, women have the attention span of two-year-olds. Women aren't the only ones with short attention spans. Men also have short attention spans, as I know, speaking for myself, it's hard for me to concentrate on a TV show without glancing at my phone or social media profiles only to look up lost as to what's going on with the TV show. This short attention span has created a flaking phenomenon today like no other. This phenomenon forced me to create a technique that allows you to confirm a date without confirming a date. I simply withhold the location of the date until the morning of the date. I do this by informing the woman to let me think of a nice location that accommodates both of us, and I'll let her know the morning of the date. You could even tell her the night before the date if you so choose. On the morning of the date, you should always ask, "Does this work for you?" after sending the location. Some guys have informed me that this still seems low value and insecure to them and that they would just simply enjoy their own company if the woman didn't arrive or flaked on the date. My rebuttal to this statement is that once you truly become a high-value male, your time means more to you than a woman's perception of you. When you're building an empire, you don't have time for flakes. That hour or two it took me to get dressed and commute to the date location means more to me than any woman's perception of me would ever mean. I'm well aware that some women might speculate that you're confirming a date by sending the location the morning of the date, or she may even make other plans since you withheld the location and she thought you flaked on her, but my top priority is to always to put my purpose first. Once you become a high-value man, a woman's perception of you is not the top priority, which is why you check her when you feel she is disrespecting you. Some men argue that checking a woman who is seemingly flirting with other men in their face is a sign of insecurity. I disagree wholeheartedly; my self-respect will always mean more to me than a woman's perception of me. Women will do things like text or talk on their phones on the date. As a man, you're damned if you do and damned if you don't, so you might as well let her know that type of behavior won't be tolerated.

72

Hypergamy Isn't Just More Money

If you're in a monogamous relationship, it's inevitable that your girl is going to have a girls' night out from time to time. If you're a confident man, this shouldn't be an issue. You must understand that no woman is ever truly off the market, and if she so happens to meet a man whom she has a high interest in, she'll undoubtedly give him her number—unless she views you as an alpha male who is doing everything right. I firmly believe that as long as a man whom a woman views as an alpha male is doing everything right, a woman will be too busy chasing his validation to cheat. I can't tell you how many women I've met over the years who lived with their boyfriend or husband. Some even informed me that I couldn't call them so as to avoid the boyfriend catching them. A lot of times, I had nothing really going for myself financially, so this was mainly physical attraction—that is, the women view me as an alpha male. The lack of financial success would've made me a sexual alpha at that point in my life. The secret to avoiding this is to always be the woman's best option, and even that might not be enough. The thing about being a purple-pill guy is that you're aware of the female nature, and you've signed up to take the risk. Women are hypergamous, but this isn't just limited to finances. Hypergamy covers all aspects of dating. It simply means a woman trades up, but this isn't limited to trading up for a better financial situation.

I've known women to leave men who were way more financially secure for guys who simply were hotter to them. This lets me know hypergamy isn't just relegated to finances but rather to what the woman values the most. For instance, a woman might marry or be in a relationship with a man who's a better provider only to leave him for a guy she finds more attractive. Some women value sex appeal over financial stability. So if you're a guy who makes a lot of money, don't think a man who makes far less than you do is incapable of taking your woman. Remember, attraction isn't just physical appearance but rather sex appeal as a whole. Hypergamy also dictates which male a woman wants to replicate. The top priority of sex is reproduction, not pleasure. When a woman sees a man whom she finds very attractive and confident, which are indicators of strength, she instinctively wants to reproduce with him. The thing is, some women value finances over sex appeal, while some women value sex appeal over finances. Women who value finances over sex appeal would never leave a man of means for sex appeal, but they would cheat, while a woman who values sex appeal over finances would leave you once she's convinced you want something more than just sex. Of course, all of this is null and void if you're in a relationship with a woman who views you as an alpha male. Outside of the pimp, the ultimate male in the hierarchy is always the all-around alpha. You may ask, "Why would the woman get into a relationship with a man she didn't find that appealing to begin with?" Well, maybe he was the best she could do at the time. That's the same reason you dated a woman you perceived as a seven for four years even though you knew she didn't knock your socks off, so to speak, or the same reason you worked that mediocre job you hated for eight years until you found a better job. A lot of people have the motto that "something is better than nothing," and while I agree with this motto, when it comes to having a job, because we all have bills and responsibilities, I can't say I agree with it when it comes to my dating life, because the more time you spend dating a woman you really aren't that into, the less time you have to meet that woman you really are into. This is why I always advise men to never date women they don't have a crazy-high initial interest in because the in time you're spending dating them, you could be out living a social life of abundance and meeting women you have a high attraction for. Just think of how many times you've gone on a date with a woman you met online only to find out she looks nothing like her pictures. That time could have been better spent hanging out and socializing with women you have a high attraction to. As a red-pill man who's not looking to get into a committed relationship anytime soon, I don't have these concerns, as I understand the female nature and choose not to deal with this. Purple-pill men, however, agree to take on these risks and must understand that when a woman goes out with her friends, you're always at the mercy of circumstances. To be honest, it doesn't have to be a girls' night out; it could just be her going to the grocery store. The fact of the matter is, making the relationship official with a woman won't protect you from the female nature. Most men try to put a ring on it or make it official to prevent other men from sleeping with their girl, when in actuality all you have done is narrow her pool of prospects. Since you're in a relationship, she might not give that guy she perceives as a six on a scale of one to ten her number now that she is in a relationship like she would have before you two became official, but she's definitely going to give that guy she views as a ten her number if she's the kind that values sex appeal. The same holds true in the finance department. She might not give that guy who looks like he makes less than you her number if she's a woman who's big on finances, but if she encounters a man she perceives as having more wealth than you, she certainly would give him her number or take his—unless she perceives you as an alpha male. Remember, how a woman views you is subject to change at any given moment. Just because she views you as an alpha male today won't mean she will next week. All this comes with the territory when you're purple pill. When a woman does have a girls' night out, you should never call to check up on her. It'll only lower her attraction, and quite frankly, it won't stop anything, as women are far better at planning than men when it comes down to infidelity. You should never ask her the next day what she and her girls did or where they went the previous night, as it'll only make you look insecure. Women are going to do what they want to do, and there's not much you really can do about it. It's quite possible that her going out is a test, and she wants to see how you handle it. You should always carry yourself as though you're her best option; therefore, you're not concerned. When you act insecure and jealous, you're subconsciously sending the signal that you think she can do better, hence why you're so frightened. Women see this type of behavior and think, "If he thinks I can do better, then maybe I can." Confidence is always an attractive trait when it comes to attracting women, but it's important tenfold in a relationship, as it shows either you genuinely believe you're entitled to her or you feel like you got lucky. No woman wants to be with a man who feels like he got lucky. Women want to feel like they got lucky, unless they're looking for a provider. This is the old-women-date-up theory. If she views you as a provider, confidence and charisma really don't matter much to her, as she views you simply as a provider. If a woman views you as a beta provider, your charisma and attractiveness only matter when she compares you to other potential beta-male providers. I won't say sex appeal doesn't matter to a woman who's looking for or views you as a beta provider, but let's just say you don't have to exactly be a ten in her eyes.

73

Alpha Male Strategies Are Not about Sleeping with the Most Women

A lot of men are confused as to what I'm really all about. Becoming a high-value male is not the best way to attract and sleep with the most women. If your sole purpose for reading this book is to sleep with the most women possible, then you really don't understand what Alpha Male Strategies are all about. The best way to sleep with the most women is to randomly approach as many women as you possibly can throughout the day. This also would require you to optimize dating apps. Although dating apps aren't the best way to meet women, it is a tool nonetheless. I won't lie to you and act like becoming a high-value male doesn't enhance your chances with women, because it does, but a high-value man doesn't have time to date a lot of women at once. From my perspective, a high-value man can only date about three women at a time before the women start to impede on his purpose in life. Although the high-value man doesn't have the time to date as many women as the low-value man does, the high-value man is in a much better place mentally because his life's happiness isn't dependent on how many women he's sleeping with at any given moment. Alpha Male Strategies are about learning to live a fulfilling life without women, not maximizing how many women you sleep with. The law of averages says that a man who approaches a one hundred women a day has a much better chance to attract and sleep with more women than the high-value man who's waiting for choosing signals does, but the guy who's waiting for choosing signals is in a much better place mentally; he's built his life to be independent of constant female validation. The guy who's waiting for choosing signals isn't waiting for them because he's afraid of rejection or thinks it's the best way to attract women; he's waiting for choosing signals because he's content in life. I tell guys regularly that I slept with more women when I lived in a basement in Brooklyn with a mattress on the floor than I do now that I have a nice, spacious apartment and am making way more money. The catch, however, was that in the past, I spent most of my time chasing women rather than my passion in life, thus why I was living in a basement. Most men who are overweight with low or no income think that they're unsuccessful with women due to their situation, but the truth is, you can attract women no matter how broke or overweight you are if you talk to enough women. The thing about becoming a high-value male is that your rejection rate greatly decreases, but be that as it may, any man, regardless of income, could attract women. The issue with most men who have some kind of insecurity is that they immediately draw the conclusion that no woman wants them after they get just a few rejections. You see, some men let their insecurities, whether it's height, their financial situation, looks, or weight, deter them from approaching more women because of a few rejections. They let rejections put them in a state of scarcity. This is very common in men who classify themselves as incels. They just gave up. Most men just don't have what it takes to withstand a lot of rejections because they take the rejections personally, when in reality, rejections have more to do with timing than anything. They find my work and immediately think that getting in the gym and pursuing your purpose in life are just about becoming more attractive to the opposite sex, when in actuality, it's more about becoming a content man than anything else. When you have a purpose in life, fitness goals, friends, and hobbies, you no longer value female validation the way you once did because you no longer have so much free time to fill. When men have a lot of free time on their hands, they usually occupy it by trying to attract women. This energy leaves you feeling depleted, as no matter how many women you attract, it'll never be enough. So to be clear, the best way to sleep with the most women is to play the numbers game, but when it's all said and done, the man who plays the number game is going to be forever chasing his tail, while the man who's pursuing his purpose is building a life of contentment void of constant female validation.

CHAPTER

74

How to Get a Threesome

Most men's number one fantasy is to have a threesome. There are a lot of variables that have to line up in order to achieve having a threesome. I don't know if there's an exact science to having threesomes, but let's just say it takes a little luck. For one, you have to have a woman who's somewhat interested in other women. The reason for this is quite simple: no matter how high a woman's interest is, she would never do it unless she finds women somewhat attractive. Just use yourself, for example. If you're a straight male, are there any circumstances in which you would perform sex acts on another man to please your woman? The only way you do that is if you found men somewhat attractive or had some kind of cuckold fetish. A cuckold is a man who gets off being submissive to his woman. This is where the luck comes into play. You have to be lucky to find a woman who is either openly bisexual or attracted to women. The next thing you need is extremely high attraction and a fear of loss. Women don't like to share their man even if they are attracted to other women. This is mainly due to the insecurities a woman has in regard to the man being more attracted to the other woman than he is to her. A woman's fear of losing you has to be greater than her fear of you finding the woman more attractive than she is. So once again, you have to have luck on your side and have a woman who isn't in a state of abundance. You simply can't give a woman who's in a state of abundance a fear of loss. If you have a woman who's in a state of scarcity, you might have a chance. You can try to put your woman in a state of scarcity by pulling back, but manipulation only works on weak-minded individuals living in scarcity. This is why the fear of loss is so important. So with this understanding, it stands to reason that the only way you'll achieve a threesome is if you've broken up with your girl before so she knows you have no problem doing it again. This leads her to do whatever it takes to keep you. With that being said, that fear of loss only works on women with some kind of scarcity mind-set. Women with a strong sense of self-worth, coupled with an abundance mind-set, no matter how high their attraction is to you, would never have a threesome with you unless it's something they've fantasized about also. This is why I say it's more about luck than anything else. You need a woman who's sexually attracted to women, has a fear of loss, and has an extremely high interest. There are circumstances where you can have women with an abundance mind-set and where you can raise her attraction so high that she falls into a scarcity mind-set, but it's extremely rare. I say that because I don't think it's possible for any woman to make me fear losing her, so it stands to reason that a lot of women could have that same mind-set. Understand that scarcity isn't about finding another man but rather about finding a man like you who just does it for her. The good news is that if you're a man who fantasizes about having a threesome, the average woman won't have that kind of abundance mind-set if you're a guy who just does it for her. This is because women have a much harder time finding men who are perfect for them. Let's be honest for a minute. Most men today are weak, and by weak, I don't mean physically; I mean mentally. Most women are able to manipulate the average man, which is not what women want. Women want a man who's able to say no and walk away if need be. A lot of men are confused as to why women are so attracted to the bad boy, but the bad boy has no problem telling a woman no. If you're dating a woman who views you as a beta male, then you shouldn't even be thinking about a threesome. When you're dating a woman who views you as a beta male, just getting sex on the regular is a challenge.

75

How to Organize Your Rotation

Once you become a high-value man, it's very important to have your rotation in order. No longer are you just able to wing it. As a high-value man with limited time, your schedule isn't flexible at all. It's your purpose first, and everything else is a distant second. With that being said, you do want to make time to socialize. I typically don't hang out with men, so in my spare time, I'm usually with women. So which woman do you see and when? Well, this is going to boil down to your schedule, but for me, I give my top girl Sundays. Sunday is typically the day I do the least work; therefore, I have more time available. I prefer not to date women during the week if I'm writing a book, but I'm willing to make accommodations if my weekend is booked and I'm genuinely interested in the woman. As the old saying goes, "people make time for the things they want to make time for." This doesn't mean I've put her ahead of my purpose, but rather I just might not have gotten as much done that particular day as I normally would. This is not exactly the end of the world. Saturday goes to the woman I like second best. I typically work half a day on Saturdays, so, therefore, my Saturday girl doesn't get the same amount of time as my Sunday girl. Working half a day isn't mandatory on my part. It's an option I have if I have nothing else to do. This isn't written in stone, however, as sometimes I take the weekends off completely.

That's an important component to the equation because as a red-pill man who's against dating monogamously, it's important that I always have prospects. I've been in the game long enough to know nothing lasts forever. A man shouldn't expect a woman to stay in his rotation forever. At some point, there's a very good chance that the women in your rotation start to push for a commitment. You might be able to string her along for a while with the old "I like to take my time" speech, but at some point, that'll probably get old. Women know their sexual market value decreases every day, and most of them are too smart to let you waste their prime sexual-market-value years on hopes and dreams. So as a red-pill man, preferably you want to have other women lined up ready to take their place. As a high-value man, your weekdays are most likely off-limits, with some exceptions, and even if they weren't, some women are only available on the weekend. This is when you should use the time before seeing the women in your rotation. Now let's suppose you didn't have any women in your rotation, and you're in the process of achieving that. In that situation, I would try to determine who my high-interest prospects are, as well as who my low-interest prospects are. When I'm referencing interest level, I'm referring to the woman's interest level in me. I would then weigh her interest level against my interest, and that tells me which woman I would see last for the evening. This is not an exact science, as I would rather date a woman last for the evening if I had an interest level of ten and her interest level in me was a six than see a woman last for the day if she had an interest of ten and I only had an interest level of six. If all things are equal, and I had the same amount of interest in both women, then I'm seeing the one who has the highest interest in me last. I do this because I know I'm closer to sleeping with her compared to the other woman. This is a rare occasion, as I'm usually already sleeping with one of the women. So I would date my low-interest prospect first, preferably around six o'clock. I would then schedule my second date for around eight thirty. I typically like to keep my dates no longer than an hour unless the chemistry is amazing. In doing so, this extra time means I don't have to rush things if things are going well. Don't feel bad dating multiple women on the same day, as a lot of women have been doing this for years. Whom do you think they're texting on the date? Their mother? I can't believe you fell for that. Women are notorious for having a man they perceive as alpha come over for a night of sex after you've dropped them off with a full belly of food and drinks you paid for. Don't get upset; they're not in a relationship with you, so they don't owe you an explanation, but you don't owe them one either. If you're a red-pill man, this is the life you chose, and thinking you're going to sleep around with multiple women while women sit around playing bingo waiting on you is ludicrous. Women always have more sex partners than men do throughout their lifetime. Look it up.

76

Hating Friends in a Relationship

Women value their friends' opinions of the men that they date. Men do also to a lesser degree. Both sexes do this because we all subconsciously know that the individual we're dating has a direct impact on our status as a whole. Women put more emphasis on their friends' opinions because they're always competing with their friends subconsciously, and the same can be said for men. Outside of the optics, what I've learned about a woman's friends' and family's perception of you really just depends on what she tells them. Now, sometimes the person you are could cause them to lose attraction, maybe because you are unemployed, financially unstable, an alcoholic, or verbally abusive. Putting those situations aside, it's usually the woman's portrayal of you that causes her friends and family to not like you. There's not much you can do to influence your woman's portrayal of you regardless of how you treat her because some women love to play the victim. They're so innocent, and you're so bad. Some men do this with their families too. If you're in this situation, just know that you have to make a choice. You can either leave the relationship, as these situations can become very uncomfortable depending on how much her friends and family come around, or you can just keep your distance. Most of you would probably choose to keep your distance, since it's not her family you're sleeping with overnight. If you're in a situation where her friends and family just don't like you for the person you are, just keep in mind that if a woman has a high-enough interest, there's nothing anybody alive could tell her to cause her to want to leave you. If she's the stubborn type, it could actually cause her to dig in just that much harder to rebel. Attraction level conquers all, and when a woman views you as an alpha male, there's usually nothing anyone could say to persuade her otherwise. If a woman views you as a beta male, then you're usually OK, as you're a "safe and reliable" choice. It's typically when a woman views you as an alpha male that this is an issue. The reason for this is that the woman throws logic to the side because of her attraction level. This loss of logic causes her to date men she otherwise wouldn't. This causes her family and friends to develop a flat-out dislike of said individual.

77

Avoiding False Rape Accusations

Before I get started with this chapter, I want to state for the record that there is not a 100 percent surefire way to prevent false rape accusations. Trying to get you locked up for something you didn't do is just wrong, and karma will be a calling on this evil woman. Just understand that the more women you sleep with, the greater the chance of you being accused falsely of rape. With that said, there are some measures you can do to limit the possibility. For starters, you have to understand that no means no. "No" doesn't mean "try harder." Now, during the seduction phase when you're trying to create an opportunity for sex, there's a very good chance you might hear "stop" or "no." When you hear those words, you should stop immediately. This doesn't mean you can't try again later, but whenever she says to stop, you should stop—no questions asked. Sometimes it's not that she doesn't want to have sex but rather that you're moving too quickly before she's ready. Whatever the case, just to be on the safe side, you should stop. When you try to progress things too quickly with women, they'll slow you down to the speed they're comfortable with. You'll know when to stop completely because she'll say "stop" or "no" in an obviously angry or irritated tone. She might leave the situation altogether if you've made her really uncomfortable. If that's the case, you've likely blown any chance of sleeping with her in the future. You should almost expect women to put up some kind of resistance when engaging in sex with you for the first time. These are objections she's having within herself. If she's put herself in a position for you to seduce her, and you're patient, there's a good chance sex will take place, but you should never force it. Always err on the side of caution if you're unsure of her temperament.

You should never sleep with an inebriated or intoxicated woman. At that point, a woman can't give you consent of her own free will. A glass of wine doesn't cause a woman to become inebriated, as I advise meeting women for a drink to keep date prices down—but a few shots of Hennessy will. Let's not kid ourselves here; every man, if he's being honest with himself, knows when a woman is not in control of her faculties. If you had to carry the woman into the house, I think it's very likely she's unable to give consent. My rule here is when in doubt, don't sleep with her. I don't care if you do feel this may be your only opportunity. It's just not worth it in my book.

If you're a single man, in a perfect world, you truly shouldn't be obligated to contact a woman again after sleeping with her. While this is true, we aren't living in a perfect world. Ghosting a woman after sex, especially if she really liked you, can cause her to seek revenge. While most women aren't this spiteful, some women will go as far as to get you locked up if you treat them this way. I've ghosted women but never right after sex. I deliberately converse back and forth with them after sex even if I know full well that I have no intention of seeing them again. This is to limit the possibility of a woman falsely accusing me. A woman scorned is a man burned. It's sad we live in a society where a simple unproven allegation could ruin a man's life, but that's what we're dealing with. The only thing we as men can do is adapt. I advise you to store all text messages you have with women. I commonly take screenshots of them and email them to myself to save storage space on my phone. This sounds kind of extreme, but every man thinks it could never happen to them until the day it does. Women legally extort rich and famous men by threatening a lawsuit that they know would ruin the man's reputation, therefore causing the man to settle out of court in order to prevent it from going public, and all the while the media protects women's identities. I always found it odd how a man could have potentially raped a woman, and she's willing to let it go for a few dollars. If someone had done something of that nature to me, I wouldn't want anything but a stiff prison sentence for them. This fact alone lets us know that a lot of these claims are false.

78

Where Will This Social Media Era End Up?

Everything has a cause and an effect. Social media has changed dating forever. Thanks to social media, every woman has the attention span of a cockroach. The reason for this is that every day, her inbox is flooded with more thirsty men vying for her sexual companionship. Men are more confused than ever as to how to maintain a woman's interest in these days of social media. This has caused more and more young men to seek answers via the internet. This thirst for answers has led more young men, and even older men, to find the red pill. The red pill is when a man is no longer ignorant of the female-male dynamic. This has led more men to become emotionally unavailable. So what's the result? Well, most women at some point mature and want to settle down and start and a family. My view is that eventually, over time, there won't be many men who are willing to settle down to be a provider. For decades now, it's been commonplace for a woman to have fun in her prime years with men she perceives as alpha males only to settle down with a naive beta-male provider who believes the woman is actually in love with him, when in actuality, he's only a disposable tool to provide for her offspring or potential offspring. Just as women have found free validation online, causing their attention span to decrease, more and more men have found the red pill, causing them to not even want monogamous relationships anymore now that they've found out about the female nature. Just as social media has caused more and more men to become frustrated with women, I think that same social media will cause a lot of female frustration in the long run. You can already find this frustration going on online in the female "dating with a purpose" movement. This movement comes from the frustration some women are already feeling due to an overwhelming majority of men not wanting anything exclusive since finding out about the female nature. This is funny, considering these same men would have been unaware of the female nature had they not first sought out answers as to why it is so hard to get or maintain a woman's interest in the first place. I expect to see more and more of these "dating with a purpose" groups from women in the future, as most men will probably be red pill by then and not want anything monogamous. If you're thinking to yourself, "There will always be a beta male waiting for her," you're probably right, but what you must understand is that just because a woman has a man doesn't mean he's necessarily the man she really wanted. I think it's fair to say that we all hate settling for someone less than what we think we deserve.

79

Leaving a Legacy

Every man wants to leave something behind so the world knows he existed. This is a natural human desire that most of us instinctively feel. This is usually done by having children. As a red-pill man myself, I'll openly admit I have thought about the possibility of having children. You must understand, however, that once you impregnate a woman, you no longer have control; she does. Men complain about family court laws, but you have no one to blame but yourself once you impregnate a woman. The same goes for men who get married. If you want to get married, get married, but don't complain if you get a divorce and get raped in family court. I quickly quash that notion, as I don't want to be a paycheck to a woman for the next eighteen years. On top of that, you put yourself in a position for the courts to tell you when you can and can't see your child. If you want to have children to leave a legacy, I truly understand, as it's a natural human instinct. Just don't complain later if things don't go your way. I'm about solutions, not bitching and complaining. There is, however, another way a man can leave a legacy, and that's with his purpose in life. Jesus Christ, Isaac Newton, Plato, Beethoven, and George Washington are just a few names of the men who never had children, but I bet you've heard of every last one of them. That is because they left an impact on society. Their impact on society will probably outlive any family heritage. For any man who finds the red or purple pill, this is always a choice that each one of us must make. If you decide to have a child, just understand the courts don't recognize financial hardships. They only recognize monthly payments. I emphasize payments, because in my estimation, it's easier than dealing with most baby mothers. As with anything, there are always outliers, but some baby mothers can be a real pain in the ass to the point where it's easier to just deal with the courts. This is a difficult decision, as most men who want to leave an impact on society won't quench their desire to leave an heir, and I understand that completely.

CHAPTER

80

What's the End Game?

If you're a red-pill man reading this, you ask yourself, "What does this all lead to?" If you're a purple-pill man, then your ultimate goal is to find a woman and settle down with. If you're a red-pill man, it can seem like your life is always going to be a revolving door of women, leaving you with an empty feeling. I understand that your purpose does help tremendously with this, but for some, it still may not be a solution by itself long term. This is why finding the red pill can be a gift and a curse. The gift is no longer being frustrated when a woman loses interest seemingly from nowhere, and the curse is not being able to let your guard down enough to ever fall completely in love again. You may love a woman again, but to be in love means to trust a woman completely with your emotions, and as a red-pill man, it's just not possible. It's sort of like America signing a treaty with North Korea. They may sign the treaty, but they'll never fully trust one another. The fact of the matter is that an overwhelming majority of men will go purple pill after being red pill. This is mainly due to a man's natural instinct to have a family. It's not natural for a man to casually sleep around forever. Most men just give up and accept women's flaws and settle down at some point, despite knowing the risk. I'm not here to tell you what's right or wrong; I'm just stating my thoughts and predictions. As for myself, I no longer get joy out of sleeping with several dozen women throughout the year anymore. It's not that I'm going purple pill, but rather I just get more joy out of my purpose than I ever did sleeping around with random women. At the same time, I do enjoy female companionship, which is why a steady rotation of two to three women works wonders for me. This provides enough variety while simultaneously providing me with female companionship when needed. I don't think I'll ever go purple pill, as the mere thought of sleeping with the same woman for an extended period of time makes me nauseous, but that's just me; every man doesn't have that same issue. Most men's biggest issue going purple pill will be trust. Most red-pill men will never trust again but would rather settle for the lesser of two evils. That's choosing between being heartbroken and never experiencing anything meaningful with a woman again. Most men have no choice in the matter, as their scarcity mind-set and limiting beliefs in themselves have relegated them to accepting their role as a beta-male provider. Men who have deemed themselves beta-male providers have no choice but to commit in order to receive any kind of female companionship. Women do not sleep with men they perceive as beta without some kind of financial incentive, and since the majority of women won't sleep with a man for cash directly, they'll do this indirectly through a mutually beneficial relationship, which is usually a man providing most of the financial support. As previously stated, every man has the choice between accepting the role of a beta-male provider and finding women who view him as an alpha male. The only thing that makes a man have a sexual market value of ten is if he thinks he's a ten. I think I'm a ten; therefore, I'm a ten. But how can that be if I can't sleep with every woman I want? It's not about sleeping with every woman; it's about accepting the fact that it's impossible for every woman to find you attractive. Once you understand that, you'll never let rejection deter you again. This fearlessness of rejection forever prohibits you from accepting a woman who views you as a beta male for anything other than a sex partner. So what's ultimately the end game? The end game is to know there's never an end game! We're all living in a social media purgatory!

Printed in Great
Britain
by Amazon

31917973R00170